MERRILL EDUCATION
WITH INTRODUCTION AND COMMENTARY BY SAMUEL T. GLADDING

A Guide to Ethical Conduct
for the Helping Professions

Second Edition

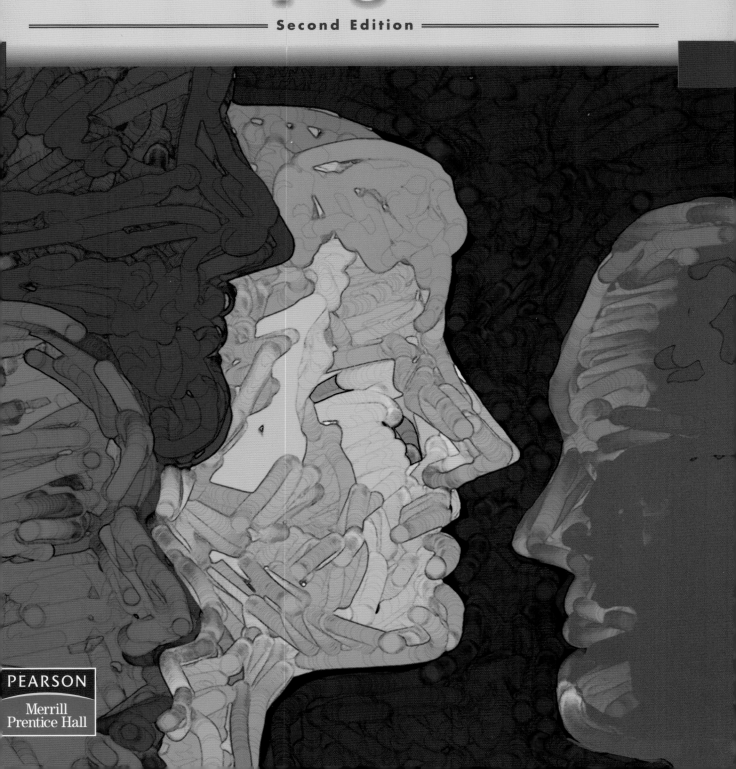

PEARSON

Merrill
Prentice Hall

A Guide to Ethical Conduct for the Helping Professions

Second Edition

Merrill Education

With Introduction and Commentary by

Samuel T. Gladding

Wake Forest University

PEARSON

Merrill
Prentice Hall

Upper Saddle River, New Jersey
Columbus, Ohio

Vice President and Executive Publisher: Jeffery W. Johnston
Publisher: Kevin M. Davis
Associate Editor: Meredith Sarver
Editorial Assistant: Sarah Kenoyer
Production Editor: Mary Harlan
Design Coordinator: Diane C. Lorenzo
Cover Design: Candace Rowley
Cover Image: SuperStock
Production Manager: Laura Messerly
Director of Marketing: David Gesell
Marketing Manager: Autumn Purdy
Marketing Coordinator: Brian Mounts

This book was printed and bound by Bind Rite Graphics. The cover was printed by The Lehigh Press, Inc.

Pearson Education Ltd.
Pearson Education Singapore Pte. Ltd.
Pearson Education Canada, Ltd.
Pearson Education–Japan

Pearson Education Australia Pty. Limited
Pearson Education North Asia Ltd.
Pearson Educación de Mexico, S.A. de C.V.
Pearson Education Malaysia Pte. Ltd.

10 9 8 7 6 5 4 3 2 1
ISBN: 0-13-239886-9

Contents

CHAPTER 1

An Overview of Ethics in the Helping Professions

The helping professions are not value-free or neutral (Corey, Corey, & Callanan, 2005; Cottone & Tarvydas, 2003; Schulte, 1990). Rather, they are based on values, which are "orienting beliefs about what is good . . . and how that good should be achieved" (Bergin, 1985, p. 99). Indeed, values are at the core of relationships and the goals of helping (Egan, 2002; Okun, 2002). In addition, because helping professions are so complex and multifaceted, human service workers, by necessity, must depend on codes of ethics for guidance and direction (Corey, Corey, & Callanan, 2007; DePauw, 1986).

Professional helpers who are not clear about their own values, ethics, and responsibilities or those of their clients can cause harm despite their best intentions (Wilcoxon, Remley, Gladding, & Huber, 2007). Therefore, it is vital for them to be knowledgeable about themselves in addition to the ethics pertaining to their professions (Sperry, 2006). Not understanding oneself or not knowing codes of ethics is inexcusable. Neither is a defense for unethical behavior (Remley & Herlihy, 2005).

This guide contains seven ethical codes and standards under which human service workers operate. However, before examining these codes, an overview of ethics in the helping professions is given. The synopsis provides a framework for examining codes of ethics in general.

DEFINITIONS: ETHICS AND MORALITY

Ethics involves "making decisions of a moral nature about people and their interaction in society" (Kitchener, 1986, p. 306). The term is often used synonymously with morality, and in some cases the two terms overlap. Both deal with "what is good and bad or the study of human conduct and values" (Van Hoose & Kottler, 1985, p. 2). Yet each has a different meaning.

Ethics is generally defined as a philosophical discipline. It is "concerned with human conduct and moral decision making" (Van Hoose & Kottler, 1985, p. 3). Ethics are normative in nature and focus on principles and standards that govern relationships between individuals, such as those between professional helpers and their clients.

Morality, on the other hand, involves judgment or evaluation of action. It is usually based within cultural contexts or religious standards (Corey et al., 2007). It is associated with such words as *good, bad, right, wrong, ought,* and *should* (Brandt,

1959; Grant, 1992). Four components to moral behavior have been defined by James Rest and translated into professional ethics by Elizabeth Welfel (2006). They are moral sensitivity, moral reasoning, moral motivation, and moral character. These characteristics of morality deal with sensitivity, thinking, decision making, and resolve or action. Professional helpers must examine all of these aspects of morality on a continuous basis. Likewise, they must scrutinize the theories they employ which have embedded within them moral presuppositions about human nature that explicitly and implicitly answer questions about morality such as "what is a person?" and "what should a person be or become?" (Christopher, 1996, p. 18).

ETHICS AND HELPING

As a group, professional helpers are concerned with the nature of ethics and values and how ethical theory can enlighten and illuminate their reasoning (Ford, 2006). Indeed, "a well-developed ethical theory is essential for practicing professionals. It provides a framework from which practitioners can reflect on the acceptability of their actions" and from which they can evaluate moral and ethical judgments (Freeman, Engels, & Altekruse, 2004, p. 164). Often, human service workers treat ethical complaints with the same seriousness that they treat lawsuits (Remley & Herlihy, 2005). However, some professionals are better informed or more attuned to ethics than others. They are the ones, who as a group, are more sensitive to and appropriate in their ethical interactions.

Patterson (1971) has observed that professional identity is related to the knowledge and practice of ethics. Welfel (2006) has added that the effectiveness of helpers is connected to their ethical knowledge and behavior as well. Those who are not well-informed may be more prone to act unethically.

UNETHICAL BEHAVIOR

Unethical behavior can take many forms. The numerous temptations common to people everywhere exist for professional helpers as well. These lures include "physical intimacy, the titillation of gossip, or the opportunity (if the gamble pays off) to advance one's career" (Welfel & Lipsitz, 1983, p. 328). Some forms of unethical behavior are obvious and willful, whereas others are more subtle and unintentional. Regardless, the harmful outcome is often the same. The following are some of the most prevalent forms of unethical behaviors in the helping professions (Levenson, 1986; Pope & Vasquez, 2005; Swanson 1983):

- Violation of confidentiality
- Exceeding one's level of professional competence
- Negligent practice
- Claiming expertise one does not possess
- Imposing one's values on a client
- Creating dependency in a client
- Sexual activity with a client
- Certain conflicts of interest, such as relationships that only benefit the helper
- Questionable financial arrangements, such as charging excessive fees
- Improper advertising

PROFESSIONAL CODES OF ETHICS AND STANDARDS

To address ethical situations and unethical behaviors, professionals in a number of human service disciplines, including those in this guide, have developed codes of ethics and standards of conduct within their associations that represent "a consensus of the membership's normative values, beliefs, and concerns about ethical behavior" (Freeman et al., 2004, p. 163). Professionals voluntarily abide by such codes for many reasons but primarily because of the strength of such documents . Yet, there are limitations to such codes, too.

Strengths of Ethical Codes

Codes of ethics have multiple strengths. The following are among the greatest strengths of these formal documents. First, ethical codes ensure the protection of "clients' rights while identifying expectations of practitioners" (Wilcoxon, 1987, p. 510). In other words, ethical codes provide some guidelines for professional behavior. Clients as well as counselors can use codes of ethics and standards as a guide in evaluating questionable treatment or requests.

A second strength of ethical codes is that without them a group of people with similar interests, skills, and backgrounds cannot be considered a professional organization (Herlihy & Corey, 2006). Thus, ethics help professionalize an association. They are also designed "to provide some guidelines for the professional behavior of members" of a group on a personal level (Swanson, 1983, p. 53).

Three other strengths of ethical codes, according to Van Hoose and Kottler (1985), are as follows:

- Ethical codes protect the profession from government. They allow the profession to regulate itself and function autonomously instead of being controlled by legislation.
- Ethical codes help control internal disagreements and bickering, thus promoting stability within the profession.
- Ethical codes protect practitioners from the public, especially in regard to malpractice suits. If professionals behave according to ethical guidelines, the behavior is judged to be in compliance with accepted standards.

Finally, ethical codes help increase public trust in the integrity of a profession and provide clients with some protection from charlatans and those who are incompetent (Vacc, Juhnke, & Nilsen, 2001). Clients can use codes of ethics and standards as a guide in evaluating questionable treatment.

Limitations of Ethical Codes

Ethical codes are not without limitations. For instance, Remley and Herlihy (2005) note that ethical codes are general and idealistic; they seldom answer specific questions. Furthermore, these documents do not address "foreseeable professional dilemmas" (Remley, 1985, p. 181). Rather, they provide guidelines, based on experiences and values, of how professionals should behave. In many ways, ethical standards represent the collected wisdom of a profession at a particular time but nothing else.

Other limitations concerning codes of ethics which are frequently mentioned (Beymer, 1971; Corey, Corey, & Callanan, 2007; Talbutt, 1981) are as follows:

- Some issues cannot be resolved by a code of ethics.
- Enforcing ethical codes is difficult; for example, there are sometimes complications in systematically bringing together the interest of all parties involved in an ethical dispute.
- There may be conflicts within the standards delineated by the code.
- Some ethical issues are not covered in codes; for example, ethical codes are not proactive documents for helping professionals decide what to do in new situations.
- What may be acceptable practice at one time may be considered unethical later.
- Sometimes conflicts arise between ethical and legal codes.
- Ethical codes may not adequately address cross-cultural or multicultural issues.

Thus, ethical codes are useful in many ways, but professionals need to be aware that they will not always find all the guidance they want when consulting them. Nevertheless, when an ethical issue arises, professionals should first consult ethical standards to see whether the situation is addressed. Likewise, when professionals realize that something is not covered in an ethics code, they should raise the issue within the association to which they belong. In this way, dialogue is begun and ethical codes evolve.

CONFLICTS WITHIN AND AMONG ETHICAL CODES

The adoption of ethical codes and the emphasis placed on them has paralleled the increased professionalism of helping. But the presence of such standards poses a potential dilemma for many helpers, for three reasons.

First, as Stadler (1986) points out, in order to act ethically, professionals must be aware of ethical codes and be able to differentiate an ethical dilemma from other types of dilemmas, a differentiation that is not always easy. For example, a person might take a stand on a controversial issue, such as homosexuality, that he or she seemingly supports with ethical principles but in reality supports only with personal beliefs or biases.

Second, sometimes different ethical principles in a code offer conflicting guidelines about what to do in a given situation (Stadler, 1986). An example is the potential conflict over confidentiality and acting in the client's best interest, where a client reveals that he or she is going to attempt to harass someone or harm himself or herself. In such a situation, the professional who keeps this information confidential may actually act against the best interests of the client and the community in which the client resides.

Third, conflicts may occur when helpers belong to two or more professional organizations whose codes of ethics differ. Take for instance the ethical codes of the American Association for Marriage and Family Therapy (AAMFT, 2001) and the American Counseling Association (ACA, 2005) regarding romantic and sexual intimacy with former clients. In the AAMFT code, intimacy with former clients is prohibited for two years following termination of therapy while in the ACA code such relationships are prohibited for five years. Professional helpers associated with both groups may become unclear and confused about how long they need wait should they develop feelings for a person they have previously seen as a client.

MAKING ETHICAL DECISIONS

Ethical decision making is sometimes not easy yet is a part of being a professional. It requires virtues such as character, integrity, and moral courage as well as knowledge (Welfel, 2006). Some helpers operate from personal ethical standards without regard to the ethical guidelines developed by their professional association(s). They usually function well until faced with a dilemma "for which there is no apparent good or best solution" (Swanson, 1983, p. 57). At such times, ethical issues arise and these individuals experience anxiety, doubt, hesitation, and confusion in determining their conduct.

In such of situations, professional helpers need to be aware of resources for ethical decision making, especially when questions arise over controversial behaviors such as setting and collecting fees or the limits of confidentiality in working with a minor. *Ethical reasoning*, "the process of determining which ethical principles are involved and then prioritizing them based on the professional requirements and beliefs," is also crucial (Lanning, 1992, p. 21).

In making ethical decisions, human service workers should take actions "based on careful, reflective thought" about responses they think are professionally right in particular situations (Tennyson & Strom, 1986, p. 298). Several ethical principles relate to the activities and ethical choices of such persons:

- *beneficence* (doing good and preventing harm),
- *nonmaleficence* (not inflicting harm),
- *autonomy* (respecting freedom of choice and self-determination),
- *justice* (fairness), and
- *fidelity* (faithfulness or honoring commitments) (Corey et al., 2007; Welfel, 2006).

All these principles involve conscious decision making by professionals throughout the helping process. Of these principles, some experts identify nonmaleficence as the primary ethical responsibility in helping. Nonmaleficence not only involves the "removal of present harm" but the "prevention of future harm, and passive avoidance of harm" (Thompson, 1990, p. 105). It is the basis on which therapists respond to clients who may endanger themselves or others and why they respond to colleagues' unethical behavior (Daniluk & Haverkamp, 1993).

OTHER GUIDELINES FOR ACTING ETHICALLY

Swanson (1983) also lists guidelines for assessing whether professional helpers act in ethically responsible ways.

The first is *personal and professional honesty*. Professional helpers need to operate openly with themselves and those with whom they work. Hidden agendas or unacknowledged feelings hinder relationships and place those who would offer assistance on shaky ethical ground. One way to overcome personal or professional honesty problems that may get in the way of acting ethically is to receive supervision (Borders & Brown, 2006).

A second guideline is *acting in the best interest of clients*. This ideal is easier to discuss than achieve. At times, a therapist may impose personal values on clients and ignore what they really want (Gladding & Hood, 1974). At other times, a professional helper may fail to recognize an emergency and too readily accept the idea that the client's best interest is served by doing nothing.

A third guideline is that professionals *act without malice or personal gain*. Some clients are difficult to like or deal with, and it is with these individuals that helpers of all kinds must be especially careful. On the other hand, care must also be given to avoid relationships with likable clients either on a personal or professional basis. Errors in judgment are likely to occur when self-interest becomes a part of the relationship with a client (St. Germaine, 1993).

A final guideline is whether a helper can *justify an action* "as the best judgment of what should be done based upon the current state of the profession" (Swanson, 1983, p. 59). To make such a decision, individuals must keep up with current trends by reading the professional literature, attending in-service workshops and conventions, and becoming actively involved in local, state, and national activities.

The ethical casebooks that most professional helping associations publish contain examples in which helpers are presented with issues and case studies of questionable ethical situations and given both guidelines and questions to reflect on in deciding what an ethical response would be. Each situation involves a standard of the ethical code of the association.

As helpful as such a casebook may be, in many situations the proper behavior is not always obvious (Wilcoxon et al., 2007). For example, the question of confidentiality in balancing the individual rights of a person with AIDS and society's right to be protected from the spread of the disease is one with which some helpers struggle (Harding, Gray, & Neal, 1993). Likewise, multiple ethical dilemmas arise in working with adult survivors of incest, including those of confidentiality and the consequences of making decisions about reporting abuse (Daniluk & Haverkamp, 1993). Therefore, when in doubt about what to do in a given situation, it is crucial for individuals in the helping professions to consult with colleagues, in addition to using principles, guidelines, casebooks, and professional codes of ethics.

SUMMARY AND CONCLUSION

Professional helpers, through their associations, have established codes of ethics to guide them in the practice of assisting others. Acting ethically is not always easy, comfortable, or clear-cut, but there are guidelines to follow in the process.

In making an ethical decision, helpers rely on personal values as well as ethical standards. They also consult professional colleagues, casebooks, and principles. It is imperative that helpers become well informed in the area of ethics for their own well-being and that of their clients. The first place to begin is to acquire an academic knowledge of ethical standards.

The ethical codes that follow should help you in this process. They reflect current conditions and are ever-evolving documents. They do not cover all situations, but they do offer help beyond that contained in helpers' personal beliefs and values. As the helping professions continue to develop, ethical codes will probably become more complicated, and enforcement procedures will become stricter. Ignorance of ethics is no excuse for any practicing human service provider. Thus, as a professional helper you need to become familiar with codes and standards of ethics, especially ones most relevant to your practice and the association to which you belong. Such knowledge will serve you well throughout your career.

REFERENCES

Bergin, A. E. (1985). Proposed values for guiding and evaluating counseling and psychotherapy. *Counseling and Values, 29,* 99–115.

Bergin, A. E. (1992). Three contributions of a spiritual perspective to counseling, psychotherapy, and behavior change. In M. T. Burke & J. G. Miranti (Eds.), *Ethical and spiritual values in counseling* (pp. 5–15). Alexandria, VA: American Counseling Association.

Beymer, L. (1971). Who killed George Washington? *Personnel and Guidance Journal, 50,* 249–253.

Borders, D., & Brown, L. (2006). *The new handbook of clinical supervision.* Mahwah, NJ: Lawrence Erlbaum.

Brandt, R. (1959). *Ethical theory.* Upper Saddle River, NJ: Prentice Hall.

Christopher, J. C. (1996). Counseling's inescapable moral visions. *Journal of Counseling & Development, 75,* 17–25.

Corey, G., Corey, M. S., & Callanan, P. (2005). An approach to teaching ethics courses in human services and counseling. *Counseling and Values, 49,* 193–207.

Corey, G., Corey, M. S., & Callanan, P. (2007). *Issues and ethics in the helping professions* (7th ed.). Pacific Grove, CA: Brooks/Cole.

Cottone, R. R., & Tarvydas, V. M. (2003). *Ethical and professional issues in counseling* (2nd ed.). Upper Saddle River, NJ: Merrill/Prentice Hall.

Daniluk, J. C., & Haverkamp, B. E. (1993). Ethical issues in counseling adult survivors of incest. *Journal of Counseling and Development, 72,* 16–22.

DePauw, M. E. (1986). Avoiding ethical violations: A timeline perspective for individual counseling. *Journal of Counseling and Development, 64,* 303–305.

Egan, G. (2002). *The skilled helper* (7th ed.). Pacific Grove, CA: Brooks/Cole.

Ford, G. G. (2006). *Ethical reasoning for mental health professionals.* Thousand Oaks, CA: Sage.

Freeman, S. J., Engels, D. W., & Altekruse, M. K. (2004). Foundations for ethical standards and codes: The role of moral philosophy and theory in ethics. *Counseling and Values, 48,* 163–173.

Gladding, S. T., & Hood, W. D. (1974). Five cents, please. *School Counselor, 21,* 40–43.

Grant, B. (1992). The moral nature of psychotherapy. In M. T. Burke & J. G. Miranti (Eds.), *Ethical and spiritual values in counseling* (pp. 27–35). Alexandria, VA: American Counseling Association.

Harding, A. K., Gray, L. A., & Neal, M. (1993). Confidentiality limits with clients who have HIV: A review of ethical and legal guidelines and professional policies. *Journal of Counseling and Development, 71,* 297–304.

Herlihy, B., & Corey, C. (2006). *ACA ethical standards casebook* (6th ed.). Alexandria, VA: American Counseling Association.

Kitchener, K. S. (1986). Teaching applied ethics in counselor education: An integration of psychological processes and philosophical analysis. *Journal of Counseling and Development, 64,* 306–310.

Kitchener, K. S. (1994, May). Doing good well: The wisdom behind ethical supervision. *Counseling and Human Development,* 1–8.

Lanning, W. (1992, December). Ethical codes and responsible decision-making. *ACA Guidepost, 35,* 21.

Levenson, J. L. (1986). When a colleague practices unethically: Guidelines for intervention. *Journal of Counseling and Development, 64,* 315–317.

Okun, B. F. (2002). *Effective helping.* Pacific Grove, CA: Brooks/Cole.

Patterson, C. H. (1971). Are ethics different in different settings? *Personnel and Guidance Journal, 50,* 254–259.

Pope, K. S., & Vasquez, M. J. T.. (2005). How to survive and thrive as a therapist. Washington, D.C.: American Psychological Association.

Remley, T. P., Jr. (1985). The law and ethical practices in elementary and middle schools. *Elementary School Guidance and Counseling, 19,* 181–189.

Remley, T. P., Jr., & Herlihy, B. (2005). *Ethical, legal, and professional issues in counseling* (2nd ed.). Upper Saddle River, NJ: Prentice Hall.

Schulte, J. M. (1990). The morality of influencing in counseling. *Counseling and Values, 34,* 103–118.

Sperry, L. (2006). *Ethical and professional issues in counseling and psychotherapy practice.* Boston: Allyn & Bacon.

St. Germaine, J. (1993). Dual relationships: What's wrong with them? *American Counselor, 2,* 25–30.

Stadler, H. (1986). Preface to the special issue. *Journal of Counseling and Development, 64,* 291.

Swanson, C. D. (1983). Ethics and the counselor. In J. A. Brown & R. H. Pate, Jr. (Eds.), *Being a counselor* (pp. 47–65). Pacific Grove, CA: Brooks/Cole.

Talbutt, L. C. (1981). Ethical standards: Assets and limitations. *Personnel and Guidance Journal, 60,* 110–112.

Tennyson, W. W., & Strom, S. M. (1986). Beyond professional standards: Developing responsibleness. *Journal of Counseling and Development, 64,* 298–302.

Thompson, A. (1990). *Guide to ethical practice in psychotherapy.* New York: Wiley.

Vacc, N. A., Juhnke, G. A., & Nilsen, K. A. (2001). Community mental health service providers' code of ethics and the *Standards for Educational and Psychological Testing. Journal of Counseling and Development, 79,* 217–224,

Van Hoose, W. H., & Kottler, J. (1985). *Ethical and legal issues in counseling and psychotherapy* (2nd ed.). San Francisco: Jossey-Bass.

Welfel, E. R. (2006). *Ethics in counseling and Psychotherapy* (3rd ed). Pacific Grove, CA: Brooks/Cole.

Welfel, E. R., & Lipsitz, N. E. (1983). Wanted: A comprehensive approach to ethics research and education. *Counselor Education and Supervision, 22,* 320–332.

Wilcoxon, S. A. (1987). Ethical standards: A study of application and utility. *Journal of Counseling and Development, 65,* 510–511.

Wilcoxon, S. A., Remley, T. P., Jr., Gladding, S. T., & Huber, C. H. (2007). *Ethical, legal and professional issues in the practice of marriage and family therapy* (4th ed.). Upper Saddle River, NJ: Pearson/Prentice Hall/Merrill.

Williams, C. B., & Freeman, L. T. (2002). Report of the ACA Ethics Committee: 2000–2001. *Journal of Counseling and Development, 80,* 251–254

CHAPTER 2

American Counseling Association Code of Ethics (2005)

The new ethics code of the American Counseling Association (ACA) is the most comprehensive the association has ever produced. It is binding on all counselors who are ACA members. The code is divided into eight (8) sections that represent the ideals that should guide counselors in their interactions with clients. These sections are:

- The Counseling Relationship
- Confidentiality, Privileged Communication, and Privacy
- Professional Responsibility
- Relationships with Other Professionals
- Evaluation, Assessment, and Interpretation
- Supervision, Training, and Teaching
- Research and Publication
- Resolving Ethical Issues

New areas in the 2005 *Code of Ethics* that distinguish it from the 1995 *Code of Ethics and Standards of Practice* include sections on potentially beneficial interactions, end-of-life care for terminally ill clients, technological applications, counselor incapacitation, historical and social prejudices in the diagnosis of pathology, and innovative theories and techniques. Also, in regard to research, the term "subjects" has been replaced by the word "participants" (Herlihy & Corey, 2006). Overall, the 2005 ACA *Code of Ethics* is much more thorough and user friendly than the 1995 *Code of Ethics and Standards of Practice*.

Reference

Herlihy, B., & Corey, G. (2006). *ACA ethical standards casebook* (6th ed.). Alexandria, VA: American Counseling Association

AMERICAN COUNSELING ASSOCIATION CODE OF ETHICS
(eff. 2005)

PREAMBLE

The American Counseling Association is an educational, scientific, and professional organization whose members work in a variety of settings and serve in multiple capacities. ACA members are dedicated to the enhancement of human development throughout the life span. Association members recognize diversity and embrace a cross cultural approach in support of the worth, dignity, potential, and uniqueness of people within their social and cultural contexts.

Professional values are an important way of living out an ethical commitment. Values inform principles. Inherently held values that guide our behaviors or exceed prescribed behaviors are deeply ingrained in the counselor and developed out of personal dedication, rather than the mandatory requirement of an external organization.

ACA CODE OF ETHICS PURPOSE

The *ACA Code of Ethics* serves five main purposes:

1. The *Code* enables the association to clarify to current and future members, and to those served by members, the nature of the ethical responsibilities held in common by its members.

2. The *Code* helps support the mission of the association.

3. The *Code* establishes principles that define ethical behavior and best practices of association members.

4. The *Code* serves as an ethical guide designed to assist members in constructing a professional course of action that best serves those utilizing counseling services and best promotes the values of the counseling profession.

5. The *Code* serves as the basis for processing of ethical complaints and inquiries initiated against members of the association.

The *ACA Code of Ethics* contains eight main sections that address the following areas:

Section A: The Counseling Relationship
Section B: Confidentiality, Privileged Communication, and Privacy
Section C: Professional Responsibility
Section D: Relationships with Other Professionals
Section E: Evaluation, Assessment, and Interpretation
Section F: Supervision, Training, and Teaching
Section G: Research and Publication
Section H: Resolving Ethical Issues

Each section of the *ACA Code of Ethics* begins with an Introduction. The introductions to each section discuss what counselors should aspire to with regard to ethical behavior and responsibility. The Introduction helps set the tone for that particular section and provides a starting point that invites reflection on the ethical mandates contained in each part of the *ACA Code of Ethics*.

When counselors are faced with ethical dilemmas that are difficult to resolve, they are expected to engage in a carefully considered ethical decision-making process. Reasonable differences of opinion can and do exist among counselors with respect to the ways in which values, ethical principles, and ethical standards would be applied when they conflict. While there is no specific ethical decision-making model that is most effective, counselors are expected to be familiar with a credible model of decision making that can bear public scrutiny and its application.

Through a chosen ethical decision-making process and evaluation of the context of the situation, counselors are empowered to make decisions that help expand the capacity of people to grow and develop.

A brief glossary is given to provide readers with a concise description of some of the terms used in the *ACA Code of Ethics*.

Section A: The Counseling Relationship

Introduction

Counselors encourage client growth and development in ways that foster the interest and welfare of clients and promote formation of healthy relationships. Counselors actively attempt to understand the diverse cultural backgrounds of the clients they serve. Counselors also explore their own cultural identities and how these affect their values and beliefs about the counseling process.

Counselors are encouraged to contribute to society by devoting a portion of their professional activity to services for which there is little or no financial return (pro bono publico).

A.1. Welfare of Those Served by Counselors

A.1.a.   *Primary Responsibility.* The primary responsibility of counselors is to respect the dignity and to promote the welfare of clients.

A.1.b.   *Records.* Counselors maintain records necessary for rendering professional services to their clients and as required by laws, regulations, or agency or institution procedures. Counselors include sufficient and timely documentation in their client records to facilitate the delivery and continuity of needed services. Counselors take reasonable steps to ensure that documentation in records accurately reflects client progress and services provided. If errors are made in client records, counselors take steps to properly note the correction of such errors according to agency or institutional policies. (See A.12.g.7., B.6., B.6.g., G.2.j.)

A.1.c. *Counseling: Plans.* Counselors and their clients work jointly in devising integrated counseling plans that offer reasonable promise of success and are consistent with abilities and circumstances of clients. Counselors and clients regularly review counseling plans to assess their continued viability and effectiveness, respecting the freedom of choice of clients. (See A.2.a., A.2.d., A.12.g.)

A.1.d. *Support Network Involvement.* Counselors recognize that support networks hold various meanings in the lives of clients and consider enlisting the support, understanding, and involvement of others (e.g., religious/spiritual/community leaders, family members, friends) as positive resources, when appropriate, with client consent.

A.1.e. *Employment Needs.* Counselors work with their clients considering employment in jobs that are consistent with the overall abilities, vocational limitations, physical restrictions, general temperament, interest and aptitude patterns, social skills, education, general qualifications, and other relevant characteristics and needs of clients. When appropriate, counselors appropriately trained in career development will assist in the placement of clients in positions that are consistent with the interest, culture, and the welfare of clients, employers, and/or the public.

A.2. Informed Consent in the Counseling Relationship

(See A.12.g., B.5., B.6.b., E.3., E.13.b., F.1.c., G.2.a.)

A.2.a. *Informed Consent.* Clients have the freedom to choose whether to enter into or remain in a counseling relationship and need adequate information about the counseling process and the counselors. Counselors have an obligation to review in writing and verbally with clients the rights and responsibilities of both the counselor and the client. Informed consent is an ongoing part of the counseling process, and counselors appropriately document discussions of informed consent throughout the counseling relationship.

A.2.b. *Types of Information Needed.* Counselors explicitly explain to clients the nature of all services provided. They inform clients about issues such as, but not limited to, the following: the purposes, goals, techniques, procedures, limitations, potential risks, and benefits of services; the counselor's qualifications, credentials, and relevant experience; continuation of services upon the incapacitation or death of a counselor; and other pertinent information. Counselors take steps to ensure that clients understand the implications of diagnosis, the intended use of tests and reports, fees, and billing arrangements. Clients have the

right to confidentiality and to be provided with an explanation of its limitations (including how supervisors and/or treatment team professionals are involved); to obtain clear information about their records; to participate in the ongoing counseling plans; and to refuse any services or modality change and to be advised of the consequences of such refusal.

A.2.c. *Developmental and Cultural Sensitivity.* Counselors communicate information in ways that are both developmentally and culturally appropriate. Counselors use clear and understandable language when discussing issues related to informed consent. When clients have difficulty understanding the language used by counselors, they provide necessary services (e.g., arranging for a qualified interpreter or translator) to ensure comprehension by clients. In collaboration with clients, counselors consider cultural implications of informed consent procedures and, where possible, counselors adjust their practices accordingly.

A.2.d. *Inability to Give Consent.* When counseling minors or persons unable to give voluntary consent, counselors seek the assent of clients to services, and include them in decision making as appropriate. Counselors recognize the need to balance the ethical rights of clients to make choices, their capacity to give consent or assent to receive services, and parental or familial legal rights and responsibilities to protect these clients and make decisions on their behalf.

A.3. Clients Served by Others

When counselors learn that their clients are in a professional relationship with another mental health professional, they request release from clients to inform the other professionals and strive to establish positive and collaborative professional relationships.

A.4. Avoiding Harm and Imposing Values

A.4.a. *Avoiding Harm.* Counselors act to avoid harming their clients, trainees, and research participants and to minimize or to remedy unavoidable or unanticipated harm.

A.4.b. *Personal Values.* Counselors are aware of their own values, attitudes, beliefs, and behaviors and avoid imposing values that are inconsistent with counseling goals. Counselors respect the diversity of clients, trainees, and research participants.

A.5. Roles and Relationships With Clients

(See F.3., F.10., G.3.)

A.5.a. *Current Clients.* Sexual or romantic counselor-client interactions or relationships with current clients, their romantic partners, or their family members are prohibited.

A.5.b. *Former Clients.* Sexual or romantic counselor-client interactions or relationships with former clients, their romantic partners, or their family members are prohibited for a period of 5 years following the last professional contact. Counselors, before engaging in sexual or romantic interactions or relationships with clients, their romantic partners, or client family members after 5 years following the last professional contact, demonstrate forethought and document (in written form) whether the interactions or relationship can be viewed as exploitive in some way and/or whether there is still potential to harm the former client; in cases of potential exploitation and/or harm, the counselor avoids entering such an interaction or relationship.

A.5.c. *Nonprofessional Interactions or Relationships (Other Than Sexual or Romantic Interactions or Relationships).* Counselor–client nonprofessional relationships with clients, former clients, their romantic partners, or their family members should be avoided, except when the interaction is potentially beneficial to the client. (See A.5.d.)

A.5.d. *Potentially Beneficial Interactions.* When a counselor-client nonprofessional interaction with a client or former client may be potentially beneficial to the client or former client, the counselor must document in case records, prior to the interaction (when feasible), the rationale for such an interaction, the potential benefit, and anticipated consequences for the client or former client and other individuals significantly involved with the client or former client. Such interactions should be initiated with appropriate client consent. Where unintentional harm occurs to the client or former client, or to an individual significantly involved with the client or former client, due to the nonprofessional interaction, the counselor must show evidence of an attempt to remedy such harm. Examples of potentially beneficial interactions include, but are not limited to, attending a formal ceremony (e.g., a wedding/ commitment ceremony or graduation); purchasing a service or product provided by a client or former client (excepting unrestricted bartering); hospital visits to an ill family member; mutual membership in a professional association, organization, or community. (See A.5.c.)

A.5.e. *Role Changes in the Professional Relationship.* When a counselor changes a role from the original or most recent contracted relationship, he or she obtains informed consent from the client and explains the right of the client to refuse services related to the change. Examples of role changes include

1. changing from individual to relationship or family counseling, or vice versa;

2. changing from a nonforensic evaluative role to a therapeutic role, or vice versa;

3. changing from a counselor to a researcher role (i.e., enlisting clients as research participants), or vice versa; and

4. changing from a counselor to a mediator role, or vice versa.

Clients must be fully informed of any anticipated consequences (e.g., financial, legal, personal, or therapeutic) of counselor role changes.

A.6. Roles and Relationships at Individual, Group, Institutional, and Societal Levels

A.6.a. *Advocacy.* When appropriate, counselors advocate at individual, group, institutional, and societal levels to examine potential barriers and obstacles that inhibit access and/or the growth and development of clients.

A.6.b. *Confidentiality and Advocacy.* Counselors obtain client consent prior to engaging in advocacy efforts on behalf of an identifiable client to improve the provision of services and to work toward removal of systemic barriers or obstacles that inhibit client access, growth, and development.

A.7. Multiple Clients

When a counselor agrees to provide counseling services to two or more persons who have a relationship, the counselor clarifies at the outset which person or persons are clients and the nature of the relationships the counselor will have with each involved person. If it becomes apparent that the counselor may be called upon to perform potentially conflicting roles, the counselor will clarify, adjust, or withdraw from roles appropriately. (See A.8.a., B.4.)

A.8. Group Work

(See B.4.a.)

A.8.a. *Screening.* Counselors screen prospective group counseling/therapy participants. To the extent possible, counselors select members whose needs and goals are compatible with goals of the group, who will not impede the group process, and whose well-being will not be jeopardized by the group experience.

A.8.b. *Protecting Clients.* In a group setting, counselors take reasonable precautions to protect clients from physical, emotional, or psychological trauma.

A.9. End-of-Life Care for Terminally Ill Clients

A.9.a. *Quality of Care.* Counselors strive to take measures that enable clients

1. to obtain high quality end-of-life care for their physical, emotional, social, and spiritual needs;

2. to exercise the highest degree of self-determination possible;

3. to be given every opportunity possible to engage in informed decision making regarding their end-of-life care; and

4. to receive complete and adequate assessment regarding their ability to make competent, rational decisions on their own behalf from a mental health professional who is experienced in end-of-life care practice.

A.9.b. *Counselor Competence, Choice, and Referral.* Recognizing the personal, moral, and competence issues related to end-of-life decisions, counselors may choose to work or not work with terminally ill clients who wish to explore their end-of-life options. Counselors provide appropriate referral information to ensure that clients receive the necessary help.

A.9.c. *Confidentiality.* Counselors who provide services to terminally ill individuals who are considering hastening their own deaths have the option of breaking or not breaking confidentiality, depending on applicable laws and the specific circumstances of the situation and after seeking consultation or supervision from appropriate professional and legal parties. (See B.5.c., B.7.c.)

A.10. Fees and Bartering

A.10.a. *Accepting Fees From Agency Clients.* Counselors refuse a private fee or other remuneration for rendering services to persons who are entitled to such services through the counselor's employing agency or institution. The policies of a particular agency may make explicit provisions for agency clients to receive counseling services from members of its staff in private practice. In such instances, the clients must be informed of other options open to them should they seek private counseling services.

A.10.b. *Establishing Fees.* In establishing fees for professional counseling services, counselors consider the financial status of clients and locality. In the event that the established fee structure is inappropriate for a client, counselors assist clients in attempting to find comparable services of acceptable cost.

A.10.c. *Nonpayment of Fees.* If counselors intend to use collection agencies or take legal measures to collect fees from clients who do not pay for services as agreed upon, they first inform clients of intended actions and offer clients the opportunity to make payment.

A.10.d. *Bartering.* Counselors may barter only if the relationship is not exploitive or harmful and does not place the counselor in an unfair advantage, if the client requests it, and if such arrangements are an accepted practice among professionals in the community. Counselors consider the cultural implications of bartering and discuss relevant concerns with clients and document such agreements in a clear written contract.

A.10.e. *Receiving Gifts.* Counselors understand the challenges of accepting gifts from clients and recognize that in some cultures, small gifts are a token of respect and showing gratitude. When determining whether or not to accept a gift from clients, counselors take into account the therapeutic relationship, the monetary value of the gift, a client's motivation for giving the gift, and the counselor's motivation for wanting or declining the gift.

A.11. Termination and Referral

A.11.a. *Abandonment Prohibited.* Counselors do not abandon or neglect clients in counseling. Counselors assist in making appropriate arrangements for the continuation of treatment, when necessary, during interruptions such as vacations, illness, and following termination.

A.11.b. *Inability to Assist Clients.* If counselors determine an inability to be of professional assistance to clients, they avoid entering or continuing counseling relationships. Counselors are knowledgeable about culturally and clinically appropriate referral resources and suggest these alternatives. If clients decline the suggested referrals, counselors should discontinue the relationship.

A.11.c. *Appropriate Termination.* Counselors terminate a counseling relationship when it becomes reasonably apparent that the client no longer needs assistance, is not likely to benefit, or is being harmed by continued counseling. Counselors may terminate counseling when in jeopardy of harm by the client, or another person with whom the client has a relationship, or when clients do not pay fees as agreed upon. Counselors provide pretermination counseling and recommend other service providers when necessary.

A.11.d. *Appropriate Transfer of Services.* When counselors transfer or refer clients to other practitioners, they ensure that appropriate clinical and administrative processes are completed and open communication is maintained with both clients and practitioners.

A.12. Technology Applications

A.12.a. *Benefits and Limitations.* Counselors inform clients of the benefits and limitations of using information technology applications in the counseling process and in business/billing procedures. Such technologies include but are not limited to computer hardware and software, telephones, the World Wide Web, the Internet, online assessment instruments and other communication devices.

A.12.b. *Technology-Assisted Services.* When providing technology-assisted distance counseling services, counselors determine that clients are intellectually, emotionally, and physically capable of using the application and that the application is appropriate for the needs of clients.

A.12.c. *Inappropriate Services.* When technology-assisted distance counseling services are deemed inappropriate by the counselor or client, counselors consider delivering services face to face.

A.12.d. *Access.* Counselors provide reasonable access to computer applications when providing technology-assisted distance counseling services.

A.12.e. *Laws and Statutes.* Counselors ensure that the use of technology does not violate the laws of any local, state, national, or international entity and observe all relevant statutes.

A.12.f. *Assistance.* Counselors seek business, legal, and technical assistance when using technology applications, particularly when the use of such applications crosses state or national boundaries.

A.12.g. *Technology and Informed Consent.* As part of the process of establishing informed consent, counselors do the following:

1. Address issues related to the difficulty of maintaining the confidentiality of electronically transmitted communications.

2. Inform clients of all colleagues, supervisors, and employees, such as Informational Technology (IT) administrators, who might have authorized or unauthorized access to electronic transmissions.

3. Urge clients to be aware of all authorized or unauthorized users including family members and fellow employees who have access to any technology clients may use in the counseling process.

4. Inform clients of pertinent legal rights and limitations governing the practice of a profession over state lines or international boundaries.

5. Use encrypted Web sites and e-mail communications to help ensure confidentiality when possible.

6. When the use of encryption is not possible, counselors notify clients of this fact and limit electronic transmissions to general communications that are not client specific.

7. Inform clients if and for how long archival storage of transaction records are maintained.

8. Discuss the possibility of technology failure and alternate methods of service delivery.

9. Inform clients of emergency procedures, such as calling 911 or a local crisis hotline, when the counselor is not available.

10. Discuss time zone differences, local customs, and cultural or language differences that might impact service delivery.

11. Inform clients when technology-assisted distance counseling services are not covered by insurance. (See A.2.)

A.12.h. *Sites on the World Wide Web.* Counselors maintaining sites on the World Wide Web (the Internet) do the following:

1. Regularly check that electronic links are working and professionally appropriate.

2. Establish ways clients can contact the counselor in case of technology failure.

3. Provide electronic links to relevant state licensure and professional certification boards to protect consumer rights and facilitate addressing ethical concerns.

4. Establish a method for verifying client identity.

5. Obtain the written consent of the legal guardian or other authorized legal representative prior to rendering services in the event the client is a minor child, an adult who is legally incompetent, or an adult incapable of giving informed consent.

6. Strive to provide a site that is accessible to persons with disabilities.

7. Strive to provide translation capabilities for clients who have a different primary language while also addressing the imperfect nature of such translations.

8. Assist clients in determining the validity and reliability of information found on the World Wide Web and other technology applications.

Section B: Confidentiality, Privileged Communication, and Privacy

Introduction

Counselors recognize that trust is a cornerstone of the counseling relationship. Counselors aspire to earn the trust of clients by creating an ongoing partnership, establishing and upholding appropriate boundaries, and maintaining confidentiality. Counselors communicate the parameters of confidentiality in a culturally competent manner.

B.1. Respecting Client Rights

B.1.a. *Multicultural/Diversity Considerations.* Counselors maintain awareness and sensitivity regarding cultural meanings of confidentiality and privacy. Counselors respect differing views toward disclosure of information. Counselors hold ongoing discussions with clients as to how, when, and with whom information is to be shared.

B.1.b. *Respect for Privacy.* Counselors respect client rights to privacy. Counselors solicit private information from clients only when it is beneficial to the counseling process.

B.1.c. *Respect for Confidentiality.* Counselors do not share confidential information without client consent or without sound legal or ethical justification.

B.1.d. *Explanation of Limitations.* At initiation and throughout the counseling process, counselors inform clients of the limitations of confidentiality and seek to identify foreseeable situations in which confidentiality must be breached. (See A.2.b.)

B.2. Exceptions

B.2.a. *Danger and Legal Requirements.* The general requirement that counselors keep information confidential does not apply when disclosure is required to protect clients or identified others from serious and foreseeable harm or when legal requirements demand that confidential information must be revealed. Counselors consult with other professionals when in doubt as to the validity of an exception. Additional considerations apply when addressing end-of-life issues. (See A.9.c.)

B.2.b. *Contagious, Life-Threatening Diseases.* When clients disclose that they have a disease commonly known to be both communicable and life threatening, counselors may be justified in disclosing information to identifiable third parties, if they are known to be at demonstrable and high risk of contracting the disease. Prior to making a disclosure, counselors confirm that there is such a diagnosis and assess the intent of clients to inform the third parties about their disease or to engage in any behaviors that may be harmful to an identifiable third party.

B.2.c. *Court-Ordered Disclosure.* When subpoenaed to release confidential or privileged information without a client's permission, counselors obtain written, informed consent from the client or take steps to prohibit the disclosure or have it limited as narrowly as possible due to potential harm to the client or counseling relationship.

B.2.d. *Minimal Disclosure.* To the extent possible, clients are informed before confidential information is disclosed and are involved in the disclosure decision-making process. When circumstances require the disclosure of confidential information, only essential information is revealed.

B.3. Information Shared With Others

B.3.a. *Subordinates.* Counselors make every effort to ensure that privacy and confidentiality of clients are maintained by subordinates, including employees, supervisees, students, clerical assistants, and volunteers. (See F.1.c.)

B.3.b. *Treatment Teams.* When client treatment involves a continued review or participation by a treatment team, the client will be informed of the team's existence and composition, information being shared, and the purposes of sharing such information.

B.3.c. *Confidential Settings.* Counselors discuss confidential information only in settings in which they can reasonably ensure client privacy.

B.3.d. *Third-Party Payers.* Counselors disclose information to third-party payers only when clients have authorized such disclosure.

B.3.e. *Transmitting Confidential Information.* Counselors take precautions to ensure the confidentiality of information transmitted through the use of computers, electronic mail, facsimile machines, telephones, voicemail, answering machines, and other electronic or computer technology. (See A.12.g.)

B.3.f. *Deceased Clients.* Counselors protect the confidentiality of deceased clients, consistent with legal requirements and agency or setting policies.

B.4. Groups and Families

B.4.a. *Group Work.* In group work, counselors clearly explain the importance and parameters of confidentiality for the specific group being entered.

B.4.b. *Couples and Family Counseling.* In couples and family counseling, counselors clearly define who is considered "the client" and discuss expectations and limitations of confidentiality. Counselors seek agreement and document in writing such agreement among all involved parties having capacity to give consent concerning each individual's right to confidentiality and any obligation to preserve the confidentiality of information known.

B.5. Clients Lacking Capacity to Give Informed Consent

B.5.a. *Responsibility to Clients.* When counseling minor clients or adult clients who lack the capacity to give voluntary, informed consent, counselors protect the confidentiality of information received in the counseling relationship as specified by federal and state laws, written policies, and applicable ethical standards.

B.5.b. *Responsibility to Parents and Legal Guardians.* Counselors inform parents and legal guardians about the role of counselors and the confidential nature of the counseling relationship. Counselors are sensitive to the cultural diversity of families and respect the inherent rights and responsibilities of parents/guardians over the welfare of their children/charges according to law. Counselors work to establish, as appropriate, collaborative relationships with parents/guardians to best serve clients.

B.5.c. *Release of Confidential Information.* When counseling minor clients or adult clients who lack the capacity to give voluntary consent to release confidential information, counselors seek permission from an appropriate third party to disclose information. In such instances, counselors inform clients consistent with their level of understanding and take culturally appropriate measures to safeguard client confidentiality.

B.6. Records

B.6.a. *Confidentiality of Records.* Counselors ensure that records are kept in a secure location and that only authorized persons have access to records.

B.6.b. *Permission to Record.* Counselors obtain permission from clients prior to recording sessions through electronic or other means.

B.6.c. *Permission to Observe.* Counselors obtain permission from clients prior to observing counseling sessions, reviewing session transcripts, or viewing recordings of sessions with supervisors, faculty, peers, or others within the training environment.

B.6.d. *Client Access.* Counselors provide reasonable access to records and copies of records when requested by competent clients. Counselors limit the access of clients to their records, or portions of their records, only when there is compelling evidence that such access would cause harm to the client. Counselors document the request of clients and the rationale for withholding some or all of the record in the files of clients. In situations involving multiple clients, counselors provide individual clients with only those parts of records that related directly to them and do not include confidential information related to any other client.

B.6.e. *Assistance With Records.* When clients request access to their records, counselors provide assistance and consultation in interpreting counseling records.

B.6.f. *Disclosure or Transfer.* Unless exceptions to confidentiality exist, counselors obtain written permission from clients to disclose or transfer records to legitimate third parties. Steps are taken to ensure that receivers of counseling records are sensitive to their confidential nature. (See A.3., E.4.)

B.6.g. *Storage and Disposal After Termination.* Counselors store records following termination of services to ensure reasonable future access, maintain records in accordance with state and federal statutes governing records, and dispose of client records and other sensitive materials in a manner that protects client confidentiality. When records are of an artistic nature, counselors obtain client (or guardian) consent with regards to handling of such records or documents. (See A.1.b.)

B.6.h. *Reasonable Precautions.* Counselors take reasonable precautions to protect client confidentiality in the event of the counselor's termination of practice, incapacity, or death. (See C.2.h.)

B.7. Research and Training

B.7.a. *Institutional Approval.* When institutional approval is required, counselors provide accurate information about their research proposals and obtain approval prior to conducting their research. They conduct research in accordance with the approved research protocol.

B.7.b. *Adherence to Guidelines.* Counselors are responsible for understanding and adhering to state, federal, agency, or institutional policies or applicable guidelines regarding confidentiality in their research practices.

B.7.c. *Confidentiality of Information Obtained in Research.* Violations of participant privacy and confidentiality are risks of participation in research involving human participants. Investigators maintain all research records in a secure manner. They explain to participants the risks of violations of privacy and confidentiality and disclose to participants any limits of confidentiality that reasonably can be expected. Regardless of the degree to which confidentiality will be maintained, investigators must disclose to participants any limits of confidentiality that reasonably can be expected. (See G.2.e.)

B.7.d. *Disclosure of Research Information.* Counselors do not disclose confidential information that reasonably could lead to the identification of a research participant unless they have obtained the prior consent of the person. Use of data derived from counseling relationships for purposes of training, research, or publication is confined to content that is disguised to ensure the anonymity of the individuals involved. (See G.2.a., G.2.d.)

B.7.e. *Agreement for Identification.* Identification of clients, students, or supervisees in a presentation or publication is permissible only when they have reviewed the material and agreed to its presentation or publication. (See G.4.d.)

B.8. Consultation

B.8.a. *Agreements.* When acting as consultants, counselors seek agreements among all parties involved concerning each individual's rights to confidentiality, the obligation of each individual to preserve confidential information, and the limits of confidentiality of information shared by others.

B.8.b. *Respect for Privacy.* Information obtained in a consulting relationship is discussed for professional purposes only with persons directly involved with the case. Written and oral reports present only data germane to the purposes of the consultation, and every effort is made to protect client identity and to avoid undue invasion of privacy.

B.8.c. *Disclosure of Confidential Information.* When consulting with colleagues, counselors do not disclose confidential information that reasonably could lead to the identification of a client or other person or organization with whom they have a confidential relationship unless they have obtained the prior consent of the person or organization or the disclosure cannot be avoided. They disclose information only to the extent necessary to achieve the purposes of the consultation. (See D.2.d.)

Section C: Professional Responsibility

Introduction

Counselors aspire to open, honest, and accurate communication in dealing with the public and other professionals. They practice in a nondiscriminatory manner within the boundaries of professional and personal competence and have a responsibility to abide by the *ACA Code of Ethics*. Counselors actively participate in local, state, and national associations that foster the development and improvement of counseling. Counselors advocate to promote change at the individual, group, institutional, and societal levels that improve the quality of life for individuals and groups and remove potential barriers to the provision or access of appropriate services being offered. Counselors have a responsibility to the public to engage in counseling practices that are based on rigorous research methodologies. In addition, counselors engage in self-care activities to maintain and promote their emotional, physical, mental, and spiritual well-being to best meet their professional responsibilities.

C.1. Knowledge of Standards

Counselors have a responsibility to read, understand, and follow the *ACA Code of Ethics* and adhere to applicable laws and regulations.

C.2. Professional Competence

C.2.a.   *Boundaries of Competence.* Counselors practice only within the boundaries of their competence, based on their education, training, supervised experience, state and national professional credentials, and appropriate professional experience. Counselors gain knowledge, personal awareness, sensitivity, and skills pertinent to working with a diverse client population. (See A.9.b., C.4.e., E.2., F.2., F.11.b.)

C.2.b.   *New Specialty Areas of Practice.* Counselors practice in specialty areas new to them only after appropriate education, training, and supervised experience. While developing skills in new specialty areas, counselors take steps to ensure the competence of their work and to protect others from possible harm. (See F.6.f.)

C.2.c.   *Qualified for Employment.* Counselors accept employment only for positions for which they are qualified by education, training, supervised experience, state and national professional credentials, and appropriate professional experience. Counselors hire for professional counseling positions only individuals who are qualified and competent for those positions.

C.2.d.   *Monitor Effectiveness.* Counselors continually monitor their effectiveness as professionals and take steps to improve when necessary. Counselors in private practice take reasonable steps to seek peer supervision as needed to evaluate their efficacy as counselors.

C.2.e.   *Consultation on Ethical Obligations.* Counselors take reasonable steps to consult with other counselors or related professionals when they have questions regarding their ethical obligations or professional practice.

C.2.f.   *Continuing Education.* Counselors recognize the need for continuing education to acquire and maintain a reasonable level of awareness of current scientific and professional information in their fields of activity. They take steps to maintain competence in the skills they use, are open to new procedures, and keep current with the diverse populations and specific populations with whom they work.

C.2.g.   *Impairment.* Counselors are alert to the signs of impairment from their own physical, mental, or emotional problems and refrain from offering or providing professional services when such impairment is likely to harm a client or others. They seek assistance for problems that reach the level of professional impairment, and, if necessary, they limit, suspend, or terminate their professional responsibilities until such time it is determined that they may safely resume their work. Counselors assist colleagues or supervisors in recognizing their own professional impairment and provide consultation and assistance when warranted with colleagues or supervisors showing signs of impairment and intervene as appropriate to prevent imminent harm to clients. (See A.11.b., F.8.b.)

C.2.h.   *Counselor Incapacitation or Termination of Practice.* When counselors leave a practice, they follow a prepared plan for transfer of clients and files. Counselors prepare and disseminate to an identified colleague or "records custodian" a plan for the transfer of clients and files in the case of their incapacitation, death, or termination of practice.

C.3. Advertising and Soliciting Clients

C.3.a.   *Accurate Advertising.* When advertising or otherwise representing their services to the public, counselors identify their credentials in an accurate manner that is not false, misleading, deceptive, or fraudulent.

C.3.b.   *Testimonials.* Counselors who use testimonials do not solicit them from current clients nor former clients nor any other persons who may be vulnerable to undue influence.

C.3.c.   *Statements by Others.* Counselors make reasonable efforts to ensure that statements made by others about them or the profession of counseling are accurate.

C.3.d.   *Recruiting Through Employment.* Counselors do not use their places of employment or institutional affiliation to recruit or gain clients, supervisees, or consultees for their private practices.

C.3.e.   *Products and Training Advertisements.* Counselors who develop products related to their profession or conduct workshops or training events ensure that the advertisements concerning these products or events are accurate and disclose adequate information for consumers to make informed choices. (See C.6.d.)

C.3.f. *Promoting to Those Served.* Counselors do not use counseling, teaching, training, or supervisory relationships to promote their products or training events in a manner that is deceptive or would exert undue influence on individuals who may be vulnerable. However, counselor educators may adopt textbooks they have authored for instructional purposes.

C.4. Professional Qualifications

C.4.a. *Accurate Representation.* Counselors claim or imply only professional qualifications actually completed and correct any known misrepresentations of their qualifications by others. Counselors truthfully represent the qualifications of their professional colleagues. Counselors clearly distinguish between paid and volunteer work experience and accurately describe their continuing education and specialized training. (See C.2.a.)

C.4.b. *Credentials.* Counselors claim only licenses or certifications that are current and in good standing.

C.4.c. *Educational Degrees.* Counselors clearly differentiate between earned and honorary degrees.

C.4.d. *Implying Doctoral-Level Competence.* Counselors clearly state their highest earned degree in counseling or closely related field. Counselors do not imply doctoral-level competence when only possessing a master's degree in counseling or a related field by referring to themselves as "Dr." in a counseling context when their doctorate is not in counseling or related field.

C.4.e. *Program Accreditation Status.* Counselors clearly state the accreditation status of their degree programs at the time the degree was earned.

C.4.f. *Professional Membership.* Counselors clearly differentiate between current, active memberships and former memberships in associations. Members of the American Counseling Association must clearly differentiate between professional membership, which implies the possession of at least a master's degree in counseling, and regular membership, which is open to individuals whose interests and activities are consistent with those of ACA but are not qualified for professional membership.

C.5. Nondiscrimination

Counselors do not condone or engage in discrimination based on age, culture, disability, ethnicity, race, religion/spirituality, gender, gender identity, sexual orientation, marital status/partnership, language preference, socioeconomic status, or any basis proscribed by law. Counselors do not discriminate against clients, students, employees, supervisees, or research participants in a manner that has a negative impact on these persons.

C.6. Public Responsibility

C.6.a. *Sexual Harassment.* Counselors do not engage in or condone sexual harassment. Sexual harassment is defined as sexual solicitation, physical advances, or verbal or nonverbal conduct that is sexual in nature, that occurs in connection with professional activities or roles, and that either

1. is unwelcome, is offensive, or creates a hostile workplace or learning environment, and counselors know or are told this; or

2. is sufficiently severe or intense to be perceived as harassment to a reasonable person in the context in which the behavior occurred.

Sexual harassment can consist of a single intense or severe act or multiple persistent or pervasive acts.

C.6.b. *Reports to Third Parties.* Counselors are accurate, honest, and objective in reporting their professional activities and judgments to appropriate third parties, including courts, health insurance companies, those who are the recipients of evaluation reports, and others. (See B.3., E.4.)

C.6.c. *Media Presentations.* When counselors provide advice or comment by means of public lectures, demonstrations, radio or television programs, prerecorded tapes, technology-based applications, printed articles, mailed material, or other media, they take reasonable precautions to ensure that

1. the statements are based on appropriate professional counseling literature and practice,

2. the statements are otherwise consistent with the *ACA Code of Ethics,* and

3. the recipients of the information are not encouraged to infer that a professional counseling relationship has been established.

C.6.d. *Exploitation of Others.* Counselors do not exploit others in their professional relationships. (See C.3.e.)

C.6.e. *Scientific Bases for Treatment Modalities.* Counselors use techniques/procedures/modalities that are grounded in theory and/or have an empirical or scientific foundation. Counselors who do not must define the techniques/procedures as "unproven" or "developing" and explain the potential risks and ethical considerations of using such techniques/procedures and take steps to protect clients from possible harm. (See A.4.a., E.5.c., E.5.d.)

C.7. Responsibility to Other Professionals

C.7.a. *Personal Public Statements.* When making personal statements in a public context, counselors clarify that they are speaking from their personal perspectives and that they are not speaking on behalf of all counselors or the profession.

Section D: Relationships With Other Professionals

Introduction

Professional counselors recognize that the quality of their interactions with colleagues can influence the quality of services provided to clients. They work to become knowledgeable about colleagues within and outside the field of counseling. Counselors develop positive working relationships and systems of communication with colleagues to enhance services to clients.

D.1. Relationships With Colleagues, Employers, and Employees

D.1.a. *Different Approaches.* Counselors are respectful of approaches to counseling services that differ from their own. Counselors are respectful of traditions and practices of other professional groups with which they work.

D.1.b. *Forming Relationships.* Counselors work to develop and strengthen interdisciplinary relations with colleagues from other disciplines to best serve clients.

D.1.c. *Interdisciplinary Teamwork.* Counselors who are members of interdisciplinary teams delivering multifaceted services to clients, keep the focus on how to best serve the clients. They participate in and contribute to decisions that affect the well-being of clients by drawing on the perspectives, values, and experiences of the counseling profession and those of colleagues from other disciplines. (See A.1.a.)

D.1.d. *Confidentiality.* When counselors are required by law, institutional policy, or extraordinary circumstances to serve in more than one role in judicial or administrative proceedings, they clarify role expectations and the parameters of confidentiality with their colleagues. (See B.1.c., B.1.d., B.2.c., B.2.d., B.3.b.)

D.1.e. *Establishing Professional and Ethical Obligations.* Counselors who are members of interdisciplinary teams clarify professional and ethical obligations of the team as a whole and of its individual members. When a team decision raises ethical concerns, counselors first attempt to resolve the concern within the team. If they cannot reach resolution among team members, counselors pursue other avenues to address their concerns consistent with client well-being.

D.1.f. *Personnel Selection and Assignment.* Counselors select competent staff and assign responsibilities compatible with their skills and experiences.

D.1.g. *Employer Policies.* The acceptance of employment in an agency or institution implies that counselors are in agreement with its general policies and principles. Coun-

selors strive to reach agreement with employers as to acceptable standards of conduct that allow for changes in institutional policy conducive to the growth and development of clients.

D.1.h. *Negative Conditions.* Counselors alert their employers of inappropriate policies and practices. They attempt to effect changes in such policies or procedures through constructive action within the organization. When such policies are potentially disruptive or damaging to clients or may limit the effectiveness of services provided and change cannot be effected, counselors take appropriate further action. Such action may include referral to appropriate certification, accreditation, or state licensure organizations, or voluntary termination of employment.

D.1.i. *Protection From Punitive Action.* Counselors take care not to harass or dismiss an employee who has acted in a responsible and ethical manner to expose inappropriate employer policies or practices.

D.2. Consultation

D.2.a. *Consultant Competency.* Counselors take reasonable steps to ensure that they have the appropriate resources and competencies when providing consultation services. Counselors provide appropriate referral resources when requested or needed. (See C.2.a.)

D.2.b. *Understanding Consultees.* When providing consultation, counselors attempt to develop with their consultees a clear understanding of problem definition, goals for change, and predicted consequences of interventions selected.

D.2.c. *Consultant Goals.* The consulting relationship is one in which consultee adaptability and growth toward self-direction are consistently encouraged and cultivated.

D.2.d. *Informed Consent in Consultation.* When providing consultation, counselors have an obligation to review, in writing and verbally, the rights and responsibilities of both counselors and consultees. Counselors use clear and understandable language to inform all parties involved about the purpose of the services to be provided, relevant costs, potential risks and benefits, and the limits of confidentiality. Working in conjunction with the consultee, counselors attempt to develop a clear definition of the problem, goals for change, and predicted consequences of interventions that are culturally responsive and appropriate to the needs of consultees. (See A.2.a., A.2.b.)

Section E: Evaluation, Assessment, and Interpretation

Introduction

Counselors use assessment instruments as one component of the counseling process, taking into account the client personal and cultural context. Counselors promote the well-being of individual clients or groups of clients by developing and using appropriate educational, psychological, and career assessment instruments.

E.1. General

E.1.a. *Assessment.* The primary purpose of educational, psychological, and career assessment is to provide measurements that are valid and reliable in either comparative or absolute terms. These include, but are not limited to, measurements of ability, personality, interest, intelligence, achievement, and performance. Counselors recognize the need to interpret the statements in this section as applying to both quantitative and qualitative assessments.

E.1.b. *Client Welfare.* Counselors do not misuse assessment results and interpretations, and they take reasonable steps to prevent others from misusing the information these techniques provide. They respect the client's right to know the results, the interpretations made, and the bases for counselors' conclusions and recommendations.

E.2. Competence to Use and Interpret Assessment Instruments

E.2.a. *Limits of Competence.* Counselors utilize only those testing and assessment services for which they have been trained and are competent. Counselors using technology assisted test interpretations are trained in the construct being measured and the specific instrument being used prior to using its technology based application. Counselors take reasonable measures to ensure the proper use of psychological and career assessment techniques by persons under their supervision. (See A.12.)

E.2.b. *Appropriate Use.* Counselors are responsible for the appropriate application, scoring, interpretation, and use of assessment instruments relevant to the needs of the client, whether they score and interpret such assessments themselves or use technology or other services.

E.2.c. *Decisions Based on Results.* Counselors responsible for decisions involving individuals or policies that are based on assessment results have a thorough understanding of educational, psychological, and career measurement, including validation criteria, assessment research, and guidelines for assessment development and use.

E.3. Informed Consent in Assessment

E.3.a. *Explanation to Clients.* Prior to assessment, counselors explain the nature and purposes of assessment and the specific use of results by potential recipients. The explanation will be given in the language of the client (or other legally authorized person on behalf of the client), unless an explicit exception has been agreed upon in advance. Counselors consider the client's personal or cultural context, the level of the client's understanding of the results, and the impact of the results on the client. (See A.2., A.12.g., F.1.c.)

E.3.b. *Recipients of Results.* Counselors consider the examinee's welfare, explicit understandings, and prior agreements in determining who receives the assessment results. Counselors include accurate and appropriate interpretations with any release of individual or group assessment results. (See B.2.c., B.5.)

E.4. Release of Data to Qualified Professionals

Counselors release assessment data in which the client is identified only with the consent of the client or the client's legal representative. Such data are released only to persons recognized by counselors as qualified to interpret the data. (See B.1., B.3., B.6.b.)

E.5. Diagnosis of Mental Disorders

E.5.a. *Proper Diagnosis.* Counselors take special care to provide proper diagnosis of mental disorders. Assessment techniques (including personal interview) used to determine client care (e.g., locus of treatment, type of treatment, or recommended follow-up) are carefully selected and appropriately used.

E.5.b. *Cultural Sensitivity.* Counselors recognize that culture affects the manner in which clients' problems are defined. Clients' socioeconomic and cultural experiences are considered when diagnosing mental disorders. (See A.2.c.)

E.5.c. *Historical and Social Prejudices in the Diagnosis of Pathology.* Counselors recognize historical and social prejudices in the misdiagnosis and pathologizing of certain individuals and groups and the role of mental health professionals in perpetuating these prejudices through diagnosis and treatment.

E.5.d. *Refraining From Diagnosis.* Counselors may refrain from making and/or reporting a diagnosis if they believe it would cause harm to the client or others.

E.6. Instrument Selection

E.6.a. *Appropriateness of Instruments.* Counselors carefully consider the validity, reliability, psychometric limitations, and appropriateness of instruments when selecting assessments.

E.6.b. *Referral Information.* If a client is referred to a third party for assessment, the counselor provides specific referral questions and sufficient objective data about the client to ensure that appropriate assessment instruments are utilized. (See A.9.b., B.3.)

E.6.c. *Culturally Diverse Populations.* Counselors are cautious when selecting assessments for culturally diverse populations to avoid the use of instruments that lack appropriate psychometric properties for the client population. (See A.2.c., E.5.b.)

E.7. Conditions of Assessment Administration

(See A.12.b., A.12.d.)

E.7.a. *Administration Conditions.* Counselors administer assessments under the same conditions that were established in their standardization. When assessments are not administered under standard conditions, as may be necessary to accommodate clients with disabilities, or when unusual behavior or irregularities occur during the administration, those conditions are noted in interpretation, and the results may be designated as invalid or of questionable validity.

E.7.b. *Technological Administration.* Counselors ensure that administration programs function properly and provide clients with accurate results when technological or other electronic methods are used for assessment administration.

E.7.c. *Unsupervised Assessments.* Unless the assessment instrument is designed, intended, and validated for self-administration and/or scoring, counselors do not permit inadequately supervised use.

E.7.d. *Disclosure of Favorable Conditions.* Prior to administration of assessments, conditions that produce most favorable assessment results are made known to the examinee.

E.8. Multicultural Issues/Diversity in Assessment

Counselors use with caution assessment techniques that were normed on populations other than that of the client. Counselors recognize the effects of age, color, culture, disability, ethnic group, gender, race, language preference, religion, spirituality, sexual orientation, and socioeconomic status on test administration and interpretation, and place test results in proper perspective with other relevant factors. (See A.2.c., E.5.b.)

E.9. Scoring and Interpretation of Assessments

E.9.a. *Reporting.* In reporting assessment results, counselors indicate reservations that exist regarding validity or reliability due to circumstances of the assessment or the inappropriateness of the norms for the person tested.

E.9.b. *Research Instruments.* Counselors exercise caution when interpreting the results of research instruments not having sufficient technical data to support respondent results. The specific purposes for the use of such instruments are stated explicitly to the examinee.

E.9.c. *Assessment Services.* Counselors who provide assessment scoring and interpretation services to support the assessment process confirm the validity of such interpretations. They accurately describe the purpose, norms, validity, reliability, and applications of the procedures and any special qualifications applicable to their use. The public offering of an automated test interpretations service is

considered a professional-to-professional consultation. The formal responsibility of the consultant is to the consultee, but the ultimate and overriding responsibility is to the client. (See D.2.)

E.10. Assessment Security

Counselors maintain the integrity and security of tests and other assessment techniques consistent with legal and contractual obligations. Counselors do not appropriate, reproduce, or modify published assessments or parts thereof without acknowledgment and permission from the publisher.

E.11. Obsolete Assessments and Outdated Results

Counselors do not use data or results from assessments that are obsolete or outdated for the current purpose. Counselors make every effort to prevent the misuse of obsolete measures and assessment data by others.

E.12. Assessment Construction

Counselors use established scientific procedures, relevant standards, and current professional knowledge for assessment design in the development, publication, and utilization of educational and psychological assessment techniques.

E.13. Forensic Evaluation: Evaluation for Legal Proceedings

E.13.a. *Primary Obligations.* When providing forensic evaluations, the primary obligation of counselors is to produce objective findings that can be substantiated based on information and techniques appropriate to the evaluation, which may include examination of the individual and/or review of records. Counselors are entitled to form professional opinions based on their professional knowledge and expertise that can be supported by the data gathered in evaluations. Counselors will define the limits of their reports or testimony, especially when an examination of the individual has not been conducted.

E.13.b. *Consent for Evaluation.* Individuals being evaluated are informed in writing that the relationship is for the purposes of an evaluation and is not counseling in nature, and entities or individuals who will receive the evaluation report are identified. Written consent to be evaluated is obtained from those being evaluated unless a court orders evaluations to be conducted without the written consent of individuals being evaluated. When children or vulnerable adults are being evaluated, informed written consent is obtained from a parent or guardian.

E.13.c. *Client Evaluation Prohibited.* Counselors do not evaluate individuals for forensic purposes they currently counsel or individuals they have counseled in the past. Counselors do not accept as counseling clients individuals they are evaluating or individuals they have evaluated in the past for forensic purposes.

E.13.d. *Avoid Potentially Harmful Relationships.* Counselors who provide forensic evaluations avoid potentially harmful professional or personal relationships with family members, romantic partners, and close friends of individuals they are evaluating or have evaluated in the past.

Section F: Supervision, Training, and Teaching

Introduction

Counselors aspire to foster meaningful and respectful professional relationships and to maintain appropriate boundaries with supervisees and students. Counselors have theoretical and pedagogical foundations for their work and aim to be fair, accurate, and honest in their assessments of counselors-in-training.

F.1. Counselor Supervision and Client Welfare

F.1.a. *Client Welfare.* A primary obligation of counseling supervisors is to monitor the services provided by other counselors or counselors-in-training. Counseling supervisors monitor client welfare and supervisee clinical performance and professional development. To fulfill these obligations, supervisors meet regularly with supervisees to review case notes, samples of clinical work, or live observations. Supervisees have a responsibility to understand and follow the *ACA Code of Ethics*.

F.1.b. *Counselor Credentials.* Counseling supervisors work to ensure that clients are aware of the qualifications of the supervisees who render services to the clients. (See A.2.b.)

F.1.c. *Informed Consent and Client Rights.* Supervisors make supervisees aware of client rights including the protection of client privacy and confidentiality in the counseling relationship. Supervisees provide clients with professional disclosure information and inform them of how the supervision process influences the limits of confidentiality. Supervisees make clients aware of who will have access to records of the counseling relationship and how these records will be used. (See A.2.b., B.1.d.)

F.2. Counselor Supervision Competence

F.2.a. *Supervisor Preparation.* Prior to offering clinical supervision services, counselors are trained in supervision methods and techniques. Counselors who offer clinical supervision services regularly pursue continuing education activities including both counseling and supervision topics and skills. (See C.2.a., C.2.f.)

F.2.b. *Multicultural Issues/Diversity in Supervision.* Counseling supervisors are aware of and address the role of multiculturalism/diversity in the supervisory relationship.

F.3. Supervisory Relationships

F.3.a. *Relationship Boundaries With Supervisees.* Counseling supervisors clearly define and maintain ethical professional, personal, and social relationships with their supervisees. Counseling supervisors avoid nonprofessional relationships with current supervisees. If supervisors must assume other professional roles (e.g., clinical and administrative supervisor, instructor) with supervisees, they work to minimize potential conflicts and explain to supervisees the expectations and responsibilities associated with each role. They do not engage in any form of nonprofessional interaction that may compromise the supervisory relationship.

F.3.b. *Sexual Relationships.* Sexual or romantic interactions or relationships with current supervisees are prohibited.

F.3.c. *Sexual Harassment.* Counseling supervisors do not condone or subject supervisees to sexual harassment. (See C.6.a.)

F.3.d. *Close Relatives and Friends.* Counseling supervisors avoid accepting close relatives, romantic partners, or friends as supervisees.

F.3.e. *Potentially Beneficial Relationships.* Counseling supervisors are aware of the power differential in their relationships with supervisees. If they believe nonprofessional relationships with a supervisee may be potentially beneficial to the supervisee, they take precautions similar to those taken by counselors when working with clients. Examples of potentially beneficial interactions or relationships include attending a formal ceremony; hospital visits; providing support during a stressful event; or mutual membership in a professional association, organization, or community. Counseling supervisors engage in open discussions with supervisees when they consider entering into relationships with them outside of their roles as clinical and/or administrative supervisors. Before engaging in nonprofessional relationships, supervisors discuss with supervisees and document the rationale for such interactions, potential benefits or drawbacks, and anticipated consequences for the supervisee. Supervisors clarify the specific nature and limitations of the additional role(s) they will have with the supervisee.

F.4. Supervisor Responsibilities

F.4.a. *Informed Consent for Supervision.* Supervisors are responsible for incorporating into their supervision the principles of informed consent and participation. Supervisors inform supervisees of the policies and procedures to which they are to adhere and the mechanisms for due process appeal of individual supervisory actions.

F.4.b. *Emergencies and Absences.* Supervisors establish and communicate to supervisees procedures for contacting them or, in their absence, alternative on-call supervisors to assist in handling crises.

F.4.c. *Standards for Supervisees.* Supervisors make their supervisees aware of professional and ethical standards and legal responsibilities. Supervisors of postdegree counselors encourage these counselors to adhere to professional standards of practice. (See C.1.)

F.4.d. *Termination of the Supervisory Relationship.* Supervisors or supervisees have the right to terminate the supervisory relationship with adequate notice. Reasons for withdrawal are provided to the other party. When cultural, clinical, or professional issues are crucial to the viability of the supervisory relationship, both parties make efforts to resolve differences. When termination is warranted, supervisors make appropriate referrals to possible alternative supervisors.

F.5. Counseling Supervision Evaluation, Remediation, and Endorsement

F.5.a. *Evaluation.* Supervisors document and provide supervisees with ongoing performance appraisal and evaluation feedback and schedule periodic formal evaluative sessions throughout the supervisory relationship.

F.5.b. *Limitations.* Through ongoing evaluation and appraisal, supervisors are aware of the limitations of supervisees that might impede performance. Supervisors assist supervisees in securing remedial assistance when needed. They recommend dismissal from training programs, applied counseling settings, or state or voluntary professional credentialing processes when those supervisees are unable to provide competent professional services. Supervisors seek consultation and document their decisions to dismiss or refer supervisees for assistance. They ensure that supervisees are aware of options available to them to address such decisions. (See C.2.g.)

F.5.c. *Counseling for Supervisees.* If supervisees request counseling, supervisors provide them with acceptable referrals. Counselors do not provide counseling services to supervisees. Supervisors address interpersonal competencies in terms of the impact of these issues on clients, the supervisory relationship, and professional functioning. (See F.3.a.)

F.5.d. *Endorsement.* Supervisors endorse supervisees for certification, licensure, employment, or completion of an academic or training program only when they believe supervisees are qualified for the endorsement. Regardless of qualifications, supervisors do not endorse supervisees whom they believe to be impaired in any way that would interfere with the performance of the duties associated with the endorsement.

F.6. Responsibilities of Counselor Educators

F.6.a. *Counselor Educators.* Counselor educators who are responsible for developing, implementing, and supervising educational programs are skilled as teachers and practitioners. They are knowledgeable regarding the ethical, legal, and regulatory aspects of the profession, are skilled in applying that knowledge, and make students and supervisees aware of their responsibilities. Counselor educators conduct counselor education and training programs in an ethical manner and serve as role models for professional behavior. (See C.1., C.2.a., C.2.c.)

F.6.b. *Infusing Multicultural Issues/Diversity.* Counselor educators infuse material related to multiculturalism/diversity into all courses and workshops for the development of professional counselors.

F.6.c. *Integration of Study and Practice.* Counselor educators establish education and training programs that integrate academic study and supervised practice.

F.6.d. *Teaching Ethics.* Counselor educators make students and supervisees aware of the ethical responsibilities and standards of the profession and the ethical responsibilities of students to the profession. Counselor educators infuse ethical considerations throughout the curriculum. (See C.1.)

F.6.e. *Peer Relationships.* Counselor educators make every effort to ensure that the rights of peers are not compromised when students or supervisees lead counseling groups or provide clinical supervision. Counselor educators take steps to ensure that students and supervisees understand they have the same ethical obligations as counselor educators, trainers, and supervisors.

F.6.f. *Innovative Theories and Techniques.* When counselor educators teach counseling techniques/procedures that are innovative, without an empirical foundation, or without a well-grounded theoretical foundation, they define the counseling techniques/procedures as "unproven" or "developing" and explain to students the potential risks and ethical considerations of using such techniques/procedures.

F.6.g. *Field Placements.* Counselor educators develop clear policies within their training programs regarding field placement and other clinical experiences. Counselor educators provide clearly stated roles and responsibilities for the student or supervisee, the site supervisor, and the program supervisor. They confirm that site supervisors are qualified to provide supervision and inform site supervisors of their professional and ethical responsibilities in this role.

F.6.h. *Professional Disclosure.* Before initiating counseling services, counselors-in-training disclose their status as students and explain how this status affects the limits of confidentiality. Counselor educators ensure that the clients at field placements are aware of the services rendered and the qualifications of the students and supervisees rendering those services. Students and supervisees obtain client permission before they use any information concerning the counseling relationship in the training process. (See A.2.b.)

F.7. Student Welfare

F.7.a. *Orientation.* Counselor educators recognize that orientation is a developmental process that continues throughout the educational and clinical training of students. Counseling faculty provide prospective students with information about the counselor education program's expectations:

1. the type and level of skill and knowledge acquisition required for successful completion of the training;

2. program training goals, objectives, and mission, and subject matter to be covered;

3. bases for evaluation;

4. training components that encourage self-growth or self-disclosure as part of the training process;

5. the type of supervision settings and requirements of the sites for required clinical field experiences;

6. student and supervisee evaluation and dismissal policies and procedures; and

7. up-to-date employment prospects for graduates.

F.7.b. *Self-Growth Experiences.* Counselor education programs delineate requirements for self-disclosure or self-growth experiences in their admission and program materials. Counselor educators use professional judgment when designing training experiences they conduct that require student and supervisee self-growth or self-disclosure. Students and supervisees are made aware of the ramifications their self-disclosure may have when counselors whose primary role as teacher, trainer, or supervisor requires acting on ethical obligations to the profession. Evaluative components of experiential training experiences explicitly delineate predetermined academic standards that are separate and do not depend on the student's level of self-disclosure. Counselor educators may require trainees to seek professional help to address any personal concerns that may be affecting their competency.

F.8. Student Responsibilities

F.8.a. *Standards for Students.* Counselors-in-training have a responsibility to understand and follow the *ACA Code of Ethics* and adhere to applicable laws, regulatory policies, and rules and policies governing professional staff behavior at the agency or placement setting. Students have the same obligation to clients as those required of professional counselors. (See C.1., H.1.)

F.8.b. *Impairment.* Counselors-in-training refrain from offering or providing counseling services when their physical, mental, or emotional problems are likely to harm a client or others. They are alert to the signs of impairment, seek assistance for problems, and notify their program supervisors when they are aware that they are unable to effectively provide services. In addition, they seek appropriate professional services for themselves to remediate the problems that are interfering with their ability to provide services to others. (See A.1., C.2.d., C.2.g.)

F.9. Evaluation and Remediation of Students

F.9.a. *Evaluation.* Counselors clearly state to students, prior to and throughout the training program, the levels of competency expected, appraisal methods, and timing of evaluations for both didactic and clinical competencies. Counselor educators provide students with ongoing performance appraisal and evaluation feedback throughout the training program.

F.9.b. *Limitations.* Counselor educators, throughout ongoing evaluation and appraisal, are aware of and address the inability of some students to achieve counseling competencies that might impede performance. Counselor educators:

1. assist students in securing remedial assistance when needed,

2. seek professional consultation and document their decision to dismiss or refer students for assistance, and

3. ensure that students have recourse in a timely manner to address decisions to require them to seek assistance or to dismiss them and provide students with due process according to institutional policies and procedures. (See C.2.g.)

F.9.c. *Counseling for Students.* If students request counseling or if counseling services are required as part of a remediation process, counselor educators provide acceptable referrals.

F.10. Roles and Relationships Between Counselor Educators and Students

F.10.a. *Sexual or Romantic Relationships.* Sexual or romantic interactions or relationships with current students are prohibited.

F.10.b. *Sexual Harassment.* Counselor educators do not condone or subject students to sexual harassment. (See C.6.a.)

F.10.c. *Relationships With Former Students.* Counselor educators are aware of the power differential in the relationship between faculty and students. Faculty members foster open discussions with former students when considering engaging in a social, sexual, or other intimate relationship. Faculty members discuss with the former student how their former relationship may affect the change in relationship.

F.10.d. *Nonprofessional Relationships.* Counselor educators avoid nonprofessional or ongoing professional relationships with students in which there is a risk of potential harm to the student or that may compromise the training experience or grades assigned. In addition, counselor educators do not accept any form of professional services, fees, commissions, reimbursement, or remuneration from a site for student or supervisee placement.

F.10.e. *Counseling Services.* Counselor educators do not serve as counselors to current students unless this is a brief role associated with a training experience.

F.10.f. *Potentially Beneficial Relationships.* Counselor educators are aware of the power differential in the relationship between faculty and students. If they believe a nonprofessional relationship with a student may be potentially beneficial to the student, they take precautions similar to those taken by counselors when working with clients. Examples of potentially beneficial interactions or relationships include, but are not limited to, attending a formal ceremony; hospital visits; providing support during a stressful event; or mutual membership in a professional association, organization, or community. Counselor educators engage in open discussions with students when they consider entering into relationships with students outside of their roles as teachers and supervisors. They discuss with students the rationale for such interactions, the potential benefits and drawbacks, and the anticipated consequences for the student. Educators clarify the specific nature and limitations of the additional role(s) they will have with the student prior to engaging in a nonprofessional relationship. Nonprofessional relationships with students should be time-limited and initiated with student consent.

F.11. Multicultural/Diversity Competence in Counselor Education and Training Programs

F.11.a. *Faculty Diversity.* Counselor educators are committed to recruiting and retaining a diverse faculty.

F.11.b. *Student Diversity.* Counselor educators actively attempt to recruit and retain a diverse student body. Counselor educators demonstrate commitment to multicultural/diversity competence by recognizing and valuing diverse cultures and types of abilities students bring to the training experience. Counselor educators provide appropriate accommodations that enhance and support diverse student well-being and academic performance.

F.11.c. *Multicultural/Diversity Competence.* Counselor educators actively infuse multicultural/diversity competency in their training and supervision practices. They actively train students to gain awareness, knowledge, and skills in the competencies of multicultural practice. Counselor educators include case examples, role-plays, discussion questions, and other classroom activities that promote and represent various cultural perspectives.

Section G: Research and Publication

Introduction

Counselors who conduct research are encouraged to contribute to the knowledge base of the profession and promote a clearer understanding of the conditions that lead to a healthy and more just society. Counselors support efforts of researchers by participating fully and willingly whenever possible. Counselors minimize bias and respect diversity in designing and implementing research programs.

G.1. Research Responsibilities

G.1.a. *Use of Human Research Participants.* Counselors plan, design, conduct, and report research in a manner that is consistent with pertinent ethical principles, federal and state laws, host institutional regulations, and scientific standards governing research with human research participants.

G.1.b. *Deviation From Standard Practice.* Counselors seek consultation and observe stringent safeguards to protect the rights of research participants when a research problem suggests a deviation from standard or acceptable practices.

G.1.c. *Independent Researchers.* When independent researchers do not have access to an Institutional Review Board (IRB), they should consult with researchers who are familiar with IRB procedures to provide appropriate safeguards.

G.1.d. *Precautions to Avoid Injury.* Counselors who conduct research with human participants are responsible for the welfare of participants throughout the research process and should take reasonable precautions to avoid causing injurious psychological, emotional, physical, or social effects to participants.

G.1.e. *Principal Researcher Responsibility.* The ultimate responsibility for ethical research practice lies with the principal researcher. All others involved in the research activities share ethical obligations and responsibility for their own actions.

G.1.f. *Minimal Interference.* Counselors take reasonable precautions to avoid causing disruptions in the lives of research participants that could be caused by their involvement in research.

G.1.g. *Multicultural/Diversity Considerations in Research.* When appropriate to research goals, counselors are sensitive to incorporating research procedures that take into account cultural considerations. They seek consultation when appropriate.

G.2. Rights of Research Participants

(See A.2, A.7.)

G.2.a. *Informed Consent in Research.* Individuals have the right to consent to become research participants. In seeking consent, counselors use language that:

1. accurately explains the purpose and procedures to be followed,

2. identifies any procedures that are experimental or relatively untried,

3. describes any attendant discomforts and risks,

4. describes any benefits or changes in individuals or organizations that might be reasonably expected,

5. discloses appropriate alternative procedures that would be advantageous for participants,

6. offers to answer any inquiries concerning the procedures,

7. describes any limitations on confidentiality,

8. describes the format and potential target audiences for the dissemination of research findings, and

9. instructs participants that they are free to withdraw their consent and to discontinue participation in the project at any time without penalty.

G.2.b. *Deception.* Counselors do not conduct research involving deception unless alternative procedures are not feasible and the prospective value of the research justifies the deception. If such deception has the potential to cause physical or emotional harm to research participants, the research is not conducted, regardless of prospective value. When the methodological requirements of a study necessitate concealment or deception, the investigator explains the reasons for this action as soon as possible during the debriefing.

G.2.c. *Student/Supervisee Participation.* Researchers who involve students or supervisees in research make clear to them that the decision regarding whether or not to participate in research activities does not affect one's academic standing or supervisory relationship. Students or supervisees who choose not to participate in educational research are provided with an appropriate alternative to fulfill their academic or clinical requirements.

G.2.d. *Client Participation.* Counselors conducting research involving clients make clear in the informed consent process that clients are free to choose whether or not to participate in research activities. Counselors take necessary precautions to protect clients from adverse consequences of declining or withdrawing from participation.

G.2.e. *Confidentiality of Information.* Information obtained about research participants during the course of an investigation is confidential. When the possibility exists that others may obtain access to such information, ethical research practice requires that the possibility, together with the plans for protecting confidentiality, be explained to participants as a part of the procedure for obtaining informed consent.

G.2.f. *Persons Not Capable of Giving Informed Consent.* When a person is not capable of giving informed consent, counselors provide an appropriate explanation to, obtain agreement for participation from, and obtain the appropriate consent of a legally authorized person.

G.2.g. *Commitments to Participants.* Counselors take reasonable measures to honor all commitments to research participants. (See A.2.c.)

G.2.h. *Explanations After Data Collection.* After data are collected, counselors provide participants with full clarification of the nature of the study to remove any misconceptions participants might have regarding the research. Where scientific or human values justify delaying or withholding information, counselors take reasonable measures to avoid causing harm.

G.2.i. *Informing Sponsors.* Counselors inform sponsors, institutions, and publication channels regarding research procedures and outcomes. Counselors ensure that appropriate bodies and authorities are given pertinent information and acknowledgement.

G.2.j. *Disposal of Research Documents and Records.* Within a reasonable period of time following the completion of a research project or study, counselors take steps to destroy records or documents (audio, video, digital, and written) containing confidential data or information that identifies research participants. When records are of an artistic nature, researchers obtain participant consent with regard to handling of such records or documents. (See B.4.a, B.4.g.)

G.3. Relationships With Research Participants (When Research Involves Intensive or Extended Interactions)

G.3.a. *Nonprofessional Relationships.* Nonprofessional relationships with research participants should be avoided.

G.3.b. *Relationships With Research Participants.* Sexual or romantic counselor–research participant interactions or relationships with current research participants are prohibited.

G.3.c. *Sexual Harassment and Research Participants.* Researchers do not condone or subject research participants to sexual harassment.

G.3.d. *Potentially Beneficial Interactions.* When a nonprofessional interaction between the researcher and the research participant may be potentially beneficial, the researcher must document, prior to the interaction (when feasible), the rationale for such an interaction, the potential benefit, and anticipated consequences for the research participant. Such interactions should be initiated with appropriate consent of the research participant. Where unintentional harm occurs to the research participant due to the nonprofessional interaction, the researcher must show evidence of an attempt to remedy such harm.

G.4. Reporting Results

G.4.a.   *Accurate Results.* Counselors plan, conduct, and report research accurately. They provide thorough discussions of the limitations of their data and alternative hypotheses. Counselors do not engage in misleading or fraudulent research, distort data, misrepresent data, or deliberately bias their results. They explicitly mention all variables and conditions known to the investigator that may have affected the outcome of a study or the interpretation of data. They describe the extent to which results are applicable for diverse populations.

G.4.b.   *Obligation to Report Unfavorable Results.* Counselors report the results of any research of professional value. Results that reflect unfavorably on institutions, programs, services, prevailing opinions, or vested interests are not withheld.

G.4.c.   *Reporting Errors.* If counselors discover significant errors in their published research, they take reasonable steps to correct such errors in a correction erratum, or through other appropriate publication means.

G.4.d.   *Identity of Participants.* Counselors who supply data, aid in the research of another person, report research results, or make original data available take due care to disguise the identity of respective participants in the absence of specific authorization from the participants to do otherwise. In situations where participants self-identify their involvement in research studies, researchers take active steps to ensure that data is adapted/changed to protect the identity and welfare of all parties and that discussion of results does not cause harm to participants.

G.4.e.   *Replication Studies.* Counselors are obligated to make available sufficient original research data to qualified professionals who may wish to replicate the study.

G.5. Publication

G.5.a.   *Recognizing Contributions.* When conducting and reporting research, counselors are familiar with and give recognition to previous work on the topic, observe copyright laws, and give full credit to those to whom credit is due.

G.5.b.   *Plagiarism.* Counselors do not plagiarize, that is, they do not present another person's work as their own work.

G.5.c.   *Review/Republication of Data or Ideas.* Counselors fully acknowledge and make editorial reviewers aware of prior publication of ideas or data where such ideas or data are submitted for review or publication.

G.5.d.   *Contributors.* Counselors give credit through joint authorship, acknowledgment, footnote statements, or other appropriate means to those who have contributed significantly to research or concept development in accordance with such contributions. The principal contributor is listed first and minor technical or professional contributions are acknowledged in notes or introductory statements.

G.5.e.   *Agreement of Contributors.* Counselors who conduct joint research with colleagues or students/supervisees establish agreements in advance regarding allocation of tasks, publication credit, and types of acknowledgement that will be received.

G.5.f.   *Student Research.* For articles that are substantially based on students course papers, projects, dissertations or theses, and on which students have been the primary contributors, they are listed as principal authors.

G.5.g.   *Duplicate Submission.* Counselors submit manuscripts for consideration to only one journal at a time. Manuscripts that are published in whole or in substantial part in another journal or published work are not submitted for publication without acknowledgment and permission from the previous publication.

G.5.h.   *Professional Review.* Counselors who review material submitted for publication, research, or other scholarly purposes respect the confidentiality and proprietary rights of those who submitted it. Counselors use care to make publication decisions based on valid and defensible standards. Counselors review article submissions in a timely manner and based on their scope and competency in research methodologies. Counselors who serve as reviewers at the request of editors or publishers make every effort to only review materials that are within their scope of competency and use care to avoid personal biases.

Section H: Resolving Ethical Issues

Introduction

Counselors behave in a legal, ethical, and moral manner in the conduct of their professional work. They are aware that client protection and trust in the profession depend on a high level of professional conduct. They hold other counselors to the same standards and are willing to take appropriate action to ensure that these standards are upheld.

Counselors strive to resolve ethical dilemmas with direct and open communication among all parties involved and seek consultation with colleagues and supervisors when necessary. Counselors incorporate ethical practice into their daily professional work. They engage in ongoing professional development regarding current topics in ethical and legal issues in counseling.

H.1. Standards and the Law

(See F.9.a.)

H.1.a. *Knowledge.* Counselors understand the *ACA Code of Ethics* and other applicable ethics codes from other professional organizations or from certification and licensure bodies of which they are members. Lack of knowledge or misunderstanding of an ethical responsibility is not a defense against a charge of unethical conduct.

H.1.b. *Conflicts Between Ethics and Laws.* If ethical responsibilities conflict with law, regulations, or other governing legal authority, counselors make known their commitment to the *ACA Code of Ethics* and take steps to resolve the conflict. If the conflict cannot be resolved by such means, counselors may adhere to the requirements of law, regulations, or other governing legal authority.

H.2. Suspected Violations

H.2.a. *Ethical Behavior Expected.* Counselors expect colleagues to adhere to the *ACA Code of Ethics.* When counselors possess knowledge that raises doubts as to whether another counselor is acting in an ethical manner, they take appropriate action. (See H.2.b., H.2.c.)

H.2.b. *Informal Resolution.* When counselors have reason to believe that another counselor is violating or has violated an ethical standard, they attempt first to resolve the issue informally with the other counselor if feasible, provided such action does not violate confidentiality rights that may be involved.

H.2.c. *Reporting Ethical Violations.* If an apparent violation has substantially harmed, or is likely to substantially harm a person or organization and is not appropriate for informal resolution or is not resolved properly, counselors take further action appropriate to the situation. Such action might include referral to state or national committees on professional ethics, voluntary national certification bodies, state licensing boards, or to the appropriate institutional authorities. This standard does not apply when an intervention would violate confidentiality rights or when counselors have been retained to review the work of another counselor whose professional conduct is in question.

H.2.d. *Consultation.* When uncertain as to whether a particular situation or course of action may be in violation of the *ACA Code of Ethics,* counselors consult with other counselors who are knowledgeable about ethics and the *ACA Code of Ethics,* with colleagues, or with appropriate authorities

H.2.e. *Organizational Conflicts.* If the demands of an organization with which counselors are affiliated pose a conflict with the *ACA Code of Ethics,* counselors specify the nature of such conflicts and express to their supervisors or other responsible officials their commitment to the *ACA Code of Ethics.* When possible, counselors work toward change within the organization to allow full adherence to the *ACA Code of Ethics.* In doing so, they address any confidentiality issues.

H.2.f. *Unwarranted Complaints.* Counselors do not initiate, participate in, or encourage the filing of ethics complaints that are made with reckless disregard or willful ignorance of facts that would disprove the allegation.

H.2.g. *Unfair Discrimination Against Complainants and Respondents.* Counselors do not deny persons employment, advancement, admission to academic or other programs, tenure, or promotion based solely upon their having made or their being the subject of an ethics complaint. This does not preclude taking action based upon the outcome of such proceedings or considering other appropriate information.

H.3. Cooperation With Ethics Committees

Counselors assist in the process of enforcing the *ACA Code of Ethics.* Counselors cooperate with investigations, proceedings, and requirements of the ACA Ethics Committee or ethics committees of other duly constituted associations or boards having jurisdiction over those charged with a violation. Counselors are familiar with the *ACA Policy and Procedures for Processing Complaints of Ethical Violations* and use it as a reference for assisting in the enforcement of the *ACA Code of Ethics.*

CHAPTER 3

Ethical Principles of Psychologists and Code of Conduct (2002)

The American Psychological Association (APA), like most professional associations, has revised its *Ethical Principles of Psychologists and Code of Conduct* a number of times. The latest version, referred to here and in the document itself, is known as the *Ethics Code*. It consists of an Introduction, a Preamble, General Principles, and specific Ethical Standards that are grouped under ten (10) broad headings.

The Introduction of this document points out the intent, organization, procedures, and application of the *Ethics Code*. It is basically an informational guide. The Preamble and General Principles are different in that they are geared to steering psychologists toward the highest ideals of the profession. These aspects of the *Ethics Code* are not enforceable but are meant to be considered when making an ethical decision.

The specific Ethical Standards are organized under the following headings:

- Resolving Ethical Issues
- Competence
- Human Relations
- Privacy and Confidentiality
- Advertising and Other Public Statements
- Record Keeping and Fees
- Education and Training
- Research and Publication
- Assessment
- Therapy

Each of these headings has anywhere from six (6) (e.g., Competence) to fifteen (15) (e.g., Research and Publication) subheadings under it. Like the other codes in this guide, the Ethical Standards point out the obligations professionals in the field of psychology are under in conducting themselves in a variety of situations.

ETHICAL PRINCIPLES OF PSYCHOLOGISTS AND CODE OF CONDUCT
(2002)

CONTENTS
INTRODUCTION AND APPLICABILITY
PREAMBLE
GENERAL PRINCIPLES
Principle A: Beneficence and Nonmaleficence
Principle B: Fidelity and Responsibility
Principle C: Integrity
Principle D: Justice
Principle E: Respect for People's Rights and Dignity
ETHICAL STANDARDS

INTRODUCTION AND APPLICABILITY

The American Psychological Association's (APA's) Ethical Principles of Psychologists and Code of Conduct (hereinafter referred to as the Ethics Code) consists of an Introduction, a Preamble, five General Principles (A – E), and specific Ethical Standards. The Introduction discusses the intent, organization, procedural considerations, and scope of application of the Ethics Code. The Preamble and General Principles are aspirational goals to guide psychologists toward the highest ideals of psychology. Although the Preamble and General Principles are not themselves enforceable rules, they should be considered by psychologists in arriving at an ethical course of action. The Ethical Standards set forth enforceable rules for conduct as psychologists. Most of the Ethical Standards are written broadly, in order to apply to psychologists in varied roles, although the application of an Ethical Standard may vary depending on the context. The Ethical Standards are not exhaustive. The fact that a given conduct is not specifically addressed by an Ethical Standard does not mean that it is necessarily either ethical or unethical.

This Ethics Code applies only to psychologists' activities that are part of their scientific, educational, or professional roles as psychologists. Areas covered include but are not limited to the clinical, counseling, and school practice of psychology; research; teaching; supervision of trainees; public service; policy development; social intervention; development of assessment instruments; conducting assessments; educational counseling; organizational consulting; forensic activities; program design and evaluation; and administration. This Ethics Code applies to these activities across a variety of contexts, such as in person, postal, telephone, internet, and other electronic transmissions. These activities shall be distinguished from the purely private conduct of psychologists, which is not within the purview of the Ethics Code.

Membership in the APA commits members and student affiliates to comply with the standards of the APA Ethics Code and to the rules and procedures used to enforce them. Lack of awareness or misunderstanding of an Ethical Standard is not itself a defense to a charge of unethical conduct.

The procedures for filing, investigating, and resolving complaints of unethical conduct are described in the current Rules and Procedures of the APA Ethics Committee. APA may impose sanctions on its members for violations of the standards of the Ethics Code, including termination of APA membership, and may notify other bodies and individuals of its actions. Actions that violate the standards of the Ethics Code may also lead to the imposition of sanctions on psychologists or students whether or not they are APA members by bodies other than APA, including state psychological associations, other professional groups, psychology boards, other state or federal agencies, and payors for health services. In addition, APA may take action against a member after his or her conviction of a felony, expulsion or suspension from an affiliated state psychological association, or suspension or loss of licensure. When the sanction to be imposed by APA is less than expulsion, the 2001 Rules and Procedures do not guarantee an opportunity for an in-person hearing, but generally provide that complaints will be resolved only on the basis of a submitted record.

The Ethics Code is intended to provide guidance for psychologists and standards of professional conduct that can be applied by the APA and by other bodies that choose to adopt them. The Ethics Code is not intended to be a basis of civil liability. Whether a psychologist has violated the Ethics Code standards does not by itself determine whether the psychologist is legally liable in a court action, whether a contract is enforceable, or whether other legal consequences occur.

The modifiers used in some of the standards of this Ethics Code (e.g., *reasonably, appropriate, potentially*) are included in the standards when they would (1) allow professional judgment on the part of psychologists, (2) eliminate injustice or inequality that would occur without the modifier, (3) ensure applicability across the broad range of activities conducted by psychologists, or (4) guard against a set of rigid rules that might be quickly outdated. As used in this Ethics Code, the term *reasonable* means the prevailing professional judgment of psychologists engaged in similar activities in similar circumstances, given the knowledge the psychologist had or should have had at the time.

In the process of making decisions regarding their professional behavior, psychologists must consider this Ethics Code in addition to applicable laws and psychology board regulations. In applying the Ethics Code to their professional work, psychologists may consider other materials and guidelines that have been adopted or endorsed by scientific and professional psychological organizations and the dictates of their own conscience, as well as consult with others within the field. If this Ethics Code establishes a higher standard of conduct than is required by law, psychologists must meet the higher ethical standard. If psychologists' ethical responsibilities conflict with law, regulations, or other governing legal authority, psychologists make known their commitment to this Ethics Code and take steps to resolve the conflict in a responsible manner. If the conflict is unresolvable via such means, psychologists may adhere to the requirements of the law, regulations, or other governing authority in keeping with basic principles of human rights.

PREAMBLE

Psychologists are committed to increasing scientific and professional knowledge of behavior and people's understanding of themselves and others and to the use of such knowledge to improve the condition of individuals, organizations, and society. Psychologists respect and protect civil and human rights and the central importance of freedom of inquiry and expression in research, teaching, and publication. They strive to help the public in developing informed judgments and choices concerning human behavior. In doing so, they perform many roles, such as researcher, educator, diagnostician, therapist, supervisor, consultant, administrator, social interventionist, and expert witness. This Ethics Code provides a common set of principles and standards upon which psychologists build their professional and scientific work.

This Ethics Code is intended to provide specific standards to cover most situations encountered by psycholo-

gists. It has as its goals the welfare and protection of the individuals and groups with whom psychologists work and the education of members, students, and the public regarding ethical standards of the discipline.

The development of a dynamic set of ethical standards for psychologists' work-related conduct requires a personal commitment and lifelong effort to act ethically; to encourage ethical behavior by students, supervisees, employees, and colleagues; and to consult with others concerning ethical problems.

GENERAL PRINCIPLES

This section consists of General Principles. General Principles, as opposed to Ethical Standards, are aspirational in nature. Their intent is to guide and inspire psychologists toward the very highest ethical ideals of the profession. General Principles, in contrast to Ethical Standards, do not represent obligations and should not form the basis for imposing sanctions. Relying upon General Principles for either of these reasons distorts both their meaning and purpose.

Principle A: Beneficence and Nonmaleficence

Psychologists strive to benefit those with whom they work and take care to do no harm. In their professional actions, psychologists seek to safeguard the welfare and rights of those with whom they interact professionally and other affected persons, and the welfare of animal subjects of research. When conflicts occur among psychologists' obligations or concerns, they attempt to resolve these conflicts in a responsible fashion that avoids or minimizes harm. Because psychologists' scientific and professional judgments and actions may affect the lives of others, they are alert to and guard against personal, financial, social, organizational, or political factors that might lead to misuse of their influence. Psychologists strive to be aware of the possible effect of their own physical and mental health on their ability to help those with whom they work.

Principle B: Fidelity and Responsibility

Psychologists establish relationships of trust with those with whom they work. They are aware of their professional and scientific responsibilities to society and to the specific communities in which they work. Psychologists uphold professional standards of conduct, clarify their professional roles and obligations, accept appropriate responsibility for their behavior, and seek to manage conflicts of interest that could lead to exploitation or harm. Psychologists consult with, refer to, or cooperate with other professionals and institutions to the extent needed to serve the best interests of those with whom they work. They are concerned about the ethical compliance of their colleagues' scientific and professional conduct. Psychologists strive to contribute a portion of their professional time for little or no compensation or personal advantage.

Principle C: Integrity

Psychologists seek to promote accuracy, honesty, and truthfulness in the science, teaching, and practice of psychology. In these activities psychologists do not steal, cheat, or engage in fraud, subterfuge, or intentional misrepresentation of fact. Psychologists strive to keep their promises and to avoid unwise or unclear commitments. In situations in which deception may be ethically justifiable to maximize benefits and minimize harm, psychologists have a serious obligation to consider the need for, the possible consequences of, and their responsibility to correct any resulting mistrust or other harmful effects that arise from the use of such techniques.

Principle D: Justice

Psychologists recognize that fairness and justice entitle all persons to access to and benefit from the contributions of psychology and to equal quality in the processes, procedures, and services being conducted by psychologists. Psychologists exercise reasonable judgment and take precautions to ensure that their potential biases, the boundaries of their competence, and the limitations of their expertise do not lead to or condone unjust practices.

Principle E: Respect for People's Rights and Dignity

Psychologists respect the dignity and worth of all people, and the rights of individuals to privacy, confidentiality, and self-determination. Psychologists are aware that special safeguards may be necessary to protect the rights and welfare of persons or communities whose vulnerabilities impair autonomous decision making. Psychologists are aware of and respect cultural, individual, and role differences, including those based on age, gender, gender identity, race, ethnicity, culture, national origin, religion, sexual orientation, disability, language, and socioeconomic status and consider these factors when working with members of such groups. Psychologists try to eliminate the effect on their work of biases based on those factors, and they do not knowingly participate in or condone activities of others based upon such prejudices.

ETHICAL STANDARDS

1. Resolving Ethical Issues

1.01 Misuse of Psychologists' Work

If psychologists learn of misuse or misrepresentation of their work, they take reasonable steps to correct or minimize the misuse or misrepresentation.

1.02 Conflicts Between Ethics and Law, Regulations, or Other Governing Legal Authority

If psychologists' ethical responsibilities conflict with law, regulations, or other governing legal authority, psychologists make known their commitment to the Ethics Code and take steps to resolve the conflict. If the conflict is unresolvable via such means, psychologists may adhere to the requirements of the law, regulations, or other governing legal authority.

1.03 Conflicts Between Ethics and Organizational Demands

If the demands of an organization with which psychologists are affiliated or for whom they are working conflict with this Ethics Code, psychologists clarify the nature of the conflict, make known their commitment to the Ethics Code, and to the extent feasible, resolve the conflict in a way that permits adherence to the Ethics Code.

1.04 Informal Resolution of Ethical Violations

When psychologists believe that there may have been an ethical violation by another psychologist, they attempt to resolve the issue by bringing it to the attention of that individual, if an informal resolution appears appropriate and the intervention does not violate any confidentiality rights that may be involved. (See also Standards 1.02, Conflicts Between Ethics and Law, Regulations, or Other Governing Legal Authority, and 1.03, Conflicts Between Ethics and Organizational Demands.)

1.05 Reporting Ethical Violations

If an apparent ethical violation has substantially harmed or is likely to substantially harm a person or organization and is not appropriate for informal resolution under Standard 1.04, Informal Resolution of Ethical Violations, or is not resolved properly in that fashion, psychologists take further action appropriate to the situation. Such action might include referral to state or national committees on professional ethics, to state licensing boards, or to the appropriate institutional authorities. This standard does not apply when an intervention would violate confidentiality rights or when psychologists have been retained to review the work of another psychologist whose professional conduct is in question. (See also Standard 1.02, Conflicts Between Ethics and Law, Regulations, or Other Governing Legal Authority.)

1.06 Cooperating With Ethics Committees

Psychologists cooperate in ethics investigations, proceedings, and resulting requirements of the APA or any affiliated state psychological association to which they belong. In doing so, they address any confidentiality issues. Failure to cooperate is itself an ethics violation. However, making a request for deferment of adjudication of an ethics complaint pending the outcome of litigation does not alone constitute noncooperation.

1.07 Improper Complaints

Psychologists do not file or encourage the filing of ethics complaints that are made with reckless disregard for or willful ignorance of facts that would disprove the allegation.

1.08 Unfair Discrimination Against Complainants and Respondents

Psychologists do not deny persons employment, advancement, admissions to academic or other programs, tenure, or promotion, based solely upon their having made or their being the subject of an ethics complaint. This does not preclude taking action based upon the outcome of such proceedings or considering other appropriate information.

2. Competence

2.01 Boundaries of Competence

(a) Psychologists provide services, teach, and conduct research with populations and in areas only within the boundaries of their competence, based on their education, training, supervised experience, consultation, study, or professional experience.

(b) Where scientific or professional knowledge in the discipline of psychology establishes that an understanding of factors associated with age, gender, gender identity, race, ethnicity, culture, national origin, religion, sexual orientation, disability, language, or socioeconomic status is essential for effective implementation of their services or research, psychologists have or obtain the training, experience, consultation, or supervision necessary to ensure the competence of their services, or they make appropriate referrals, except as provided in Standard 2.02, Providing Services in Emergencies.

(c) Psychologists planning to provide services, teach, or conduct research involving populations, areas, techniques, or technologies new to them undertake relevant education, training, supervised experience, consultation, or study.

(d) When psychologists are asked to provide services to individuals for whom appropriate mental health services are not available and for which psychologists have not obtained the competence necessary, psychologists with closely related prior training or experience may provide such services in order to ensure that services are not denied if they make a reasonable effort to obtain the competence required by using relevant research, training, consultation, or study.

(e) In those emerging areas in which generally recognized standards for preparatory training do not yet exist, psychologists nevertheless take reasonable steps to ensure the competence of their work and to protect clients/patients, students, supervisees, research participants, organizational clients, and others from harm.

(f) When assuming forensic roles, psychologists are or become reasonably familiar with the judicial or administrative rules governing their roles.

2.02 Providing Services in Emergencies

In emergencies, when psychologists provide services to individuals for whom other mental health services are not available and for which psychologists have not obtained the necessary training, psychologists may provide such services in order to ensure that services are not denied. The services are discontinued as soon as the emergency has ended or appropriate services are available.

2.03 Maintaining Competence

Psychologists undertake ongoing efforts to develop and maintain their competence.

2.04 Bases for Scientific and Professional Judgments

Psychologists' work is based upon established scientific and professional knowledge of the discipline. (See also Standards 2.01e, Boundaries of Competence, and 10.01b, Informed Consent to Therapy.)

2.05 Delegation of Work to Others

Psychologists who delegate work to employees, supervisees, or research or teaching assistants or who use the services of others, such as interpreters, take reasonable steps to (1) avoid delegating such work to persons who have a multiple relationship with those being served that would likely lead to exploitation or loss of objectivity; (2) authorize only those responsibilities that such persons can be expected to perform competently on the basis of their education, training, or experience, either independently or with the level of supervision being provided; and (3) see that such persons perform these services competently. (See also Standards 2.02, Providing Services in Emergencies; 3.05, Multiple Relationships; 4.01, Maintaining Confidentiality; 9.01, Bases for Assessments; 9.02, Use of Assessments; 9.03, Informed Consent in Assessments; and 9.07, Assessment by Unqualified Persons.)

2.06 Personal Problems and Conflicts

(a) Psychologists refrain from initiating an activity when they know or should know that there is a substantial likelihood that their personal problems will prevent them from performing their work-related activities in a competent manner.

(b) When psychologists become aware of personal problems that may interfere with their performing work-related duties adequately, they take appropriate measures, such as obtaining professional consultation or assistance, and determine whether they should limit, suspend, or terminate their work-related duties. (See also Standard 10.10, Terminating Therapy.)

3. Human Relations

3.01 Unfair Discrimination

In their work-related activities, psychologists do not engage in unfair discrimination based on age, gender, gender identity, race, ethnicity, culture, national origin, religion, sexual orientation, disability, socioeconomic status, or any basis proscribed by law.

3.02 Sexual Harassment

Psychologists do not engage in sexual harassment. Sexual harassment is sexual solicitation, physical advances, or verbal or nonverbal conduct that is sexual in nature, that occurs in connection with the psychologist's activities or roles as a psychologist, and that either (1) is unwelcome, is offensive, or creates a hostile workplace or educational environment, and the psychologist knows or is told this or (2) is sufficiently severe or intense to be abusive to a reasonable person in the context. Sexual harassment can consist of a single intense or severe act or of multiple persistent or pervasive acts. (See also Standard 1.08, Unfair Discrimination Against Complainants and Respondents.)

3.03 Other Harassment

Psychologists do not knowingly engage in behavior that is harassing or demeaning to persons with whom they interact in their work based on factors such as those persons' age, gender, gender identity, race, ethnicity, culture, national origin, religion, sexual orientation, disability, language, or socioeconomic status.

3.04 Avoiding Harm

Psychologists take reasonable steps to avoid harming their clients/patients, students, supervisees, research participants, organizational clients, and others with whom they work, and to minimize harm where it is foreseeable and unavoidable.

3.05 Multiple Relationships

(a) A multiple relationship occurs when a psychologist is in a professional role with a person and (1) at the same time is in another role with the same person, (2) at the same time is in a relationship with a person closely associated with or related to the person with whom the psychologist has the professional relationship, or (3) promises to enter into another relationship in the future with the person or a person closely associated with or related to the person. A psychologist refrains from entering into a multiple relationship if the multiple relationship could reasonably be expected to impair the psychologist's objectivity, competence, or effectiveness in performing his or her functions as a psychologist, or otherwise risks exploitation or harm to the person with whom the professional relationship exists. Multiple relationships that would not reasonably be expected to cause impairment or risk exploitation or harm are not unethical.

(b) If a psychologist finds that, due to unforeseen factors, a potentially harmful multiple relationship has arisen, the psychologist takes reasonable steps to resolve it with due regard for the best interests of the affected person and maximal compliance with the Ethics Code.

(c) When psychologists are required by law, institutional policy, or extraordinary circumstances to serve in more

than one role in judicial or administrative proceedings, at the outset they clarify role expectations and the extent of confidentiality and thereafter as changes occur. (See also Standards 3.04, Avoiding Harm, and 3.07, Third-Party Requests for Services.)

3.06 Conflict of Interest

Psychologists refrain from taking on a professional role when personal, scientific, professional, legal, financial, or other interests or relationships could reasonably be expected to (1) impair their objectivity, competence, or effectiveness in performing their functions as psychologists or (2) expose the person or organization with whom the professional relationship exists to harm or exploitation.

3.07 Third-Party Requests for Services

When psychologists agree to provide services to a person or entity at the request of a third party, psychologists attempt to clarify at the outset of the service the nature of the relationship with all individuals or organizations involved. This clarification includes the role of the psychologist (e.g., therapist, consultant, diagnostician, or expert witness), an identification of who is the client, the probable uses of the services provided or the information obtained, and the fact that there may be limits to confidentiality. (See also Standards 3.05, Multiple Relationships, and 4.02, Discussing the Limits of Confidentiality.)

3.08 Exploitative Relationships

Psychologists do not exploit persons over whom they have supervisory, evaluative, or other authority such as clients/patients, students, supervisees, research participants, and employees. (See also Standards 3.05, Multiple Relationships; 6.04, Fees and Financial Arrangements; 6.05, Barter With Clients/Patients; 7.07, Sexual Relationships With Students and Supervisees; 10.05, Sexual Intimacies With Current Therapy Clients/Patients; 10.06, Sexual Intimacies With Relatives or Significant Others of Current Therapy Clients/Patients; 10.07, Therapy With Former Sexual Partners; and 10.08, Sexual Intimacies With Former Therapy Clients/Patients.)

3.09 Cooperation With Other Professionals

When indicated and professionally appropriate, psychologists cooperate with other professionals in order to serve their clients/patients effectively and appropriately. (See also Standard 4.05, Disclosures.)

3.10 Informed Consent

(a) When psychologists conduct research or provide assessment, therapy, counseling, or consulting services in person or via electronic transmission or other forms of communication, they obtain the informed consent of the individual or individuals using language that is reasonably understandable to that person or persons except when conducting such activities without consent is mandated by law or governmental regulation or as otherwise provided in this Ethics Code. (See also Standards 8.02, Informed

Consent to Research; 9.03, Informed Consent in Assessments; and 10.01, Informed Consent to Therapy.)

(b) For persons who are legally incapable of giving informed consent, psychologists nevertheless (1) provide an appropriate explanation, (2) seek the individual's assent, (3) consider such persons' preferences and best interests, and (4) obtain appropriate permission from a legally authorized person, if such substitute consent is permitted or required by law. When consent by a legally authorized person is not permitted or required by law, psychologists take reasonable steps to protect the individual's rights and welfare.

(c) When psychological services are court ordered or otherwise mandated, psychologists inform the individual of the nature of the anticipated services, including whether the services are court ordered or mandated and any limits of confidentiality, before proceeding.

(d) Psychologists appropriately document written or oral consent, permission, and assent. (See also Standards 8.02, Informed Consent to Research; 9.03, Informed Consent in Assessments; and 10.01, Informed Consent to Therapy.)

3.11 Psychological Services Delivered To or Through Organizations

(a) Psychologists delivering services to or through organizations provide information beforehand to clients and when appropriate those directly affected by the services about (1) the nature and objectives of the services, (2) the intended recipients, (3) which of the individuals are clients, (4) the relationship the psychologist will have with each person and the organization, (5) the probable uses of services provided and information obtained, (6) who will have access to the information, and (7) limits of confidentiality. As soon as feasible, they provide information about the results and conclusions of such services to appropriate persons.

(b) If psychologists will be precluded by law or by organizational roles from providing such information to particular individuals or groups, they so inform those individuals or groups at the outset of the service.

3.12 Interruption of Psychological Services

Unless otherwise covered by contract, psychologists make reasonable efforts to plan for facilitating services in the event that psychological services are interrupted by factors such as the psychologist's illness, death, unavailability, relocation, or retirement or by the client's/patient's relocation or financial limitations. (See also Standard 6.02c, Maintenance, Dissemination, and Disposal of Confidential Records of Professional and Scientific Work.)

4. Privacy and Confidentiality

4.01 Maintaining Confidentiality

Psychologists have a primary obligation and take reasonable precautions to protect confidential information obtained through or stored in any medium, recognizing that the extent and limits of confidentiality may be regulated by law or established by institutional rules or professional or scientific relationship. (See also Standard 2.05, Delegation of Work to Others.)

4.02 Discussing the Limits of Confidentiality

(a) Psychologists discuss with persons (including, to the extent feasible, persons who are legally incapable of giving informed consent and their legal representatives) and organizations with whom they establish a scientific or professional relationship (1) the relevant limits of confidentiality and (2) the foreseeable uses of the information generated through their psychological activities. (See also Standard 3.10, Informed Consent.)

(b) Unless it is not feasible or is contraindicated, the discussion of confidentiality occurs at the outset of the relationship and thereafter as new circumstances may warrant.

(c) Psychologists who offer services, products, or information via electronic transmission inform clients/patients of the risks to privacy and limits of confidentiality.

4.03 Recording

Before recording the voices or images of individuals to whom they provide services, psychologists obtain permission from all such persons or their legal representatives. (See also Standards 8.03, Informed Consent for Recording Voices and Images in Research; 8.05, Dispensing With Informed Consent for Research; and 8.07, Deception in Research.)

4.04 Minimizing Intrusions on Privacy

(a) Psychologists include in written and oral reports and consultations, only information germane to the purpose for which the communication is made.

(b) Psychologists discuss confidential information obtained in their work only for appropriate scientific or professional purposes and only with persons clearly concerned with such matters.

4.05 Disclosures

(a) Psychologists may disclose confidential information with the appropriate consent of the organizational client, the individual client/patient, or another legally authorized person on behalf of the client/patient unless prohibited by law.

(b) Psychologists disclose confidential information without the consent of the individual only as mandated by law, or where permitted by law for a valid purpose such as to (1) provide needed professional services; (2) obtain appropriate professional consultations; (3) protect the client/patient, psychologist, or others from harm; or (4) obtain payment for services from a client/patient, in which instance disclosure is limited to the minimum that is necessary to achieve the purpose. (See also Standard 6.04e, Fees and Financial Arrangements.)

4.06 Consultations

When consulting with colleagues, (1) psychologists do not disclose confidential information that reasonably could lead to the identification of a client/patient, research participant, or other person or organization with whom they have a confidential relationship unless they have obtained the prior consent of the person or organization or the disclosure cannot be avoided, and (2) they disclose information only to the extent necessary to achieve the purposes of the consultation. (See also Standard 4.01, Maintaining Confidentiality.)

4.07 Use of Confidential Information for Didactic or Other Purposes

Psychologists do not disclose in their writings, lectures, or other public media, confidential, personally identifiable information concerning their clients/patients, students, research participants, organizational clients, or other recipients of their services that they obtained during the course of their work, unless (1) they take reasonable steps to disguise the person or organization, (2) the person or organization has consented in writing, or (3) there is legal authorization for doing so.

5. Advertising and Other Public Statements

5.01 Avoidance of False or Deceptive Statements

(a) Public statements include but are not limited to paid or unpaid advertising, product endorsements, grant applications, licensing applications, other credentialing applications, brochures, printed matter, directory listings, personal resumes or curricula vitae, or comments for use in media such as print or electronic transmission, statements in legal proceedings, lectures and public oral presentations, and published materials. Psychologists do not knowingly make public statements that are false, deceptive, or fraudulent concerning their research, practice, or other work activities or those of persons or organizations with which they are affiliated.

(b) Psychologists do not make false, deceptive, or fraudulent statements concerning (1) their training, experience, or competence; (2) their academic degrees; (3) their credentials; (4) their institutional or association affiliations; (5) their services; (6) the scientific or clinical basis for, or results or degree of success of, their services; (7) their fees; or (8) their publications or research findings.

(c) Psychologists claim degrees as credentials for their health services only if those degrees (1) were earned from a regionally accredited educational institution or (2) were the basis for psychology licensure by the state in which they practice.

5.02 Statements by Others

(a) Psychologists who engage others to create or place public statements that promote their professional practice, products, or activities retain professional responsibility for such statements.

(b) Psychologists do not compensate employees of press, radio, television, or other communication media in return for publicity in a news item. (See also Standard 1.01, Misuse of Psychologists' Work.)

(c) A paid advertisement relating to psychologists' activities must be identified or clearly recognizable as such.

5.03 Descriptions of Workshops and Non-Degree-Granting Educational Programs

To the degree to which they exercise control, psychologists responsible for announcements, catalogs, brochures, or advertisements describing workshops, seminars, or other non-degree-granting educational programs ensure that they accurately describe the audience for which the program is intended, the educational objectives, the presenters, and the fees involved.

5.04 Media Presentations

When psychologists provide public advice or comment via print, internet, or other electronic transmission, they take precautions to ensure that statements (1) are based on their professional knowledge, training, or experience in accord with appropriate psychological literature and practice; (2) are otherwise consistent with this Ethics Code; and (3) do not indicate that a professional relationship has been established with the recipient. (See also Standard 2.04, Bases for Scientific and Professional Judgments.)

5.05 Testimonials

Psychologists do not solicit testimonials from current therapy clients/patients or other persons who because of their particular circumstances are vulnerable to undue influence.

5.06 In-Person Solicitation

Psychologists do not engage, directly or through agents, in uninvited in-person solicitation of business from actual or potential therapy clients/patients or other persons who because of their particular circumstances are vulnerable to undue influence. However, this prohibition does not preclude (1) attempting to implement appropriate collateral contacts for the purpose of benefiting an already engaged therapy client/patient or (2) providing disaster or community outreach services.

6. Record Keeping and Fees

6.01 Documentation of Professional and Scientific Work and Maintenance of Records

Psychologists create, and to the extent the records are under their control, maintain, disseminate, store, retain, and dispose of records and data relating to their professional and scientific work in order to (1) facilitate provision of services later by them or by other professionals, (2) allow for replication of research design and analyses, (3) meet institutional requirements, (4) ensure accuracy of billing and payments, and (5) ensure compliance with law. (See also Standard 4.01, Maintaining Confidentiality.)

6.02 Maintenance, Dissemination, and Disposal of Confidential Records of Professional and Scientific Work

(a) Psychologists maintain confidentiality in creating, storing, accessing, transferring, and disposing of records under their control, whether these are written, automated, or in any other medium. (See also Standards 4.01, Maintaining Confidentiality, and 6.01, Documentation of Professional and Scientific Work and Maintenance of Records.)

(b) If confidential information concerning recipients of psychological services is entered into databases or systems of records available to persons whose access has not been consented to by the recipient, psychologists use coding or other techniques to avoid the inclusion of personal identifiers.

(c) Psychologists make plans in advance to facilitate the appropriate transfer and to protect the confidentiality of records and data in the event of psychologists' withdrawal from positions or practice. (See also Standards 3.12, Interruption of Psychological Services, and 10.09, Interruption of Therapy.)

6.03 Withholding Records for Nonpayment

Psychologists may not withhold records under their control that are requested and needed for a client's/patient's emergency treatment solely because payment has not been received.

6.04 Fees and Financial Arrangements

(a) As early as is feasible in a professional or scientific relationship, psychologists and recipients of psychological services reach an agreement specifying compensation and billing arrangements.

(b) Psychologists' fee practices are consistent with law.

(c) Psychologists do not misrepresent their fees.

(d) If limitations to services can be anticipated because of limitations in financing, this is discussed with the recipient of services as early as is feasible. (See also Standards 10.09, Interruption of Therapy, and 10.10, Terminating Therapy.)

(e) If the recipient of services does not pay for services as agreed, and if psychologists intend to use collection agencies or legal measures to collect the fees, psychologists first inform the person that such measures will be taken and provide that person an opportunity to make prompt payment. (See also Standards 4.05, Disclosures; 6.03, With-

holding Records for Nonpayment; and 10.01, Informed Consent to Therapy.)

6.05 Barter With Clients/Patients

Barter is the acceptance of goods, services, or other nonmonetary remuneration from clients/patients in return for psychological services. Psychologists may barter only if (1) it is not clinically contraindicated, and (2) the resulting arrangement is not exploitative. (See also Standards 3.05, Multiple Relationships, and 6.04, Fees and Financial Arrangements.)

6.06 Accuracy in Reports to Payors and Funding Sources

In their reports to payors for services or sources of research funding, psychologists take reasonable steps to ensure the accurate reporting of the nature of the service provided or research conducted, the fees, charges, or payments, and where applicable, the identity of the provider, the findings, and the diagnosis. (See also Standards 4.01, Maintaining Confidentiality; 4.04, Minimizing Intrusions on Privacy; and 4.05, Disclosures.)

6.07 Referrals and Fees

When psychologists pay, receive payment from, or divide fees with another professional, other than in an employer-employee relationship, the payment to each is based on the services provided (clinical, consultative, administrative, or other) and is not based on the referral itself. (See also Standard 3.09, Cooperation With Other Professionals.)

7. Education and Training

7.01 Design of Education and Training Programs

Psychologists responsible for education and training programs take reasonable steps to ensure that the programs are designed to provide the appropriate knowledge and proper experiences, and to meet the requirements for licensure, certification, or other goals for which claims are made by the program. (See also Standard 5.03, Descriptions of Workshops and Non-Degree-Granting Educational Programs.)

7.02 Descriptions of Education and Training Programs

Psychologists responsible for education and training programs take reasonable steps to ensure that there is a current and accurate description of the program content (including participation in required course- or program-related counseling, psychotherapy, experiential groups, consulting projects, or community service), training goals and objectives, stipends and benefits, and requirements that must be met for satisfactory completion of the program. This information must be made readily available to all interested parties.

7.03 Accuracy in Teaching

(a) Psychologists take reasonable steps to ensure that course syllabi are accurate regarding the subject matter to be covered, bases for evaluating progress, and the nature of course experiences. This standard does not preclude an instructor from modifying course content or requirements when the instructor considers it pedagogically necessary or desirable, so long as students are made aware of these modifications in a manner that enables them to fulfill course requirements. (See also Standard 5.01, Avoidance of False or Deceptive Statements.)

(b) When engaged in teaching or training, psychologists present psychological information accurately. (See also Standard 2.03, Maintaining Competence.)

7.04 Student Disclosure of Personal Information

Psychologists do not require students or supervisees to disclose personal information in course- or program-related activities, either orally or in writing, regarding sexual history, history of abuse and neglect, psychological treatment, and relationships with parents, peers, and spouses or significant others except if (1) the program or training facility has clearly identified this requirement in its admissions and program materials or (2) the information is necessary to evaluate or obtain assistance for students whose personal problems could reasonably be judged to be preventing them from performing their training- or professionally related activities in a competent manner or posing a threat to the students or others.

7.05 Mandatory Individual or Group Therapy

(a) When individual or group therapy is a program or course requirement, psychologists responsible for that program allow students in undergraduate and graduate programs the option of selecting such therapy from practitioners unaffiliated with the program. (See also Standard 7.02, Descriptions of Education and Training Programs.)

(b) Faculty who are or are likely to be responsible for evaluating students' academic performance do not themselves provide that therapy. (See also Standard 3.05, Multiple Relationships.)

7.06 Assessing Student and Supervisee Performance

(a) In academic and supervisory relationships, psychologists establish a timely and specific process for providing feedback to students and supervisees. Information regarding the process is provided to the student at the beginning of supervision.

(b) Psychologists evaluate students and supervisees on the basis of their actual performance on relevant and established program requirements.

7.07 Sexual Relationships With Students and Supervisees

Psychologists do not engage in sexual relationships with students or supervisees who are in their department, agency, or training center or over whom psychologists have or are likely to have evaluative authority. (See also Standard 3.05, Multiple Relationships.)

8. Research and Publication

8.01 Institutional Approval

When institutional approval is required, psychologists provide accurate information about their research proposals and obtain approval prior to conducting the research. They conduct the research in accordance with the approved research protocol.

8.02 Informed Consent to Research

(a) When obtaining informed consent as required in Standard 3.10, Informed Consent, psychologists inform participants about (1) the purpose of the research, expected duration, and procedures; (2) their right to decline to participate and to withdraw from the research once participation has begun; (3) the foreseeable consequences of declining or withdrawing; (4) reasonably foreseeable factors that may be expected to influence their willingness to participate such as potential risks, discomfort, or adverse effects; (5) any prospective research benefits; (6) limits of confidentiality; (7) incentives for participation; and (8) whom to contact for questions about the research and research participants' rights. They provide opportunity for the prospective participants to ask questions and receive answers. (See also Standards 8.03, Informed Consent for Recording Voices and Images in Research; 8.05, Dispensing With Informed Consent for Research; and 8.07, Deception in Research.)

(b) Psychologists conducting intervention research involving the use of experimental treatments clarify to participants at the outset of the research (1) the experimental nature of the treatment; (2) the services that will or will not be available to the control group(s) if appropriate; (3) the means by which assignment to treatment and control groups will be made; (4) available treatment alternatives if an individual does not wish to participate in the research or wishes to withdraw once a study has begun; and (5) compensation for or monetary costs of participating including, if appropriate, whether reimbursement from the participant or a third-party payor will be sought. (See also Standard 8.02a, Informed Consent to Research.)

8.03 Informed Consent for Recording Voices and Images in Research

Psychologists obtain informed consent from research participants prior to recording their voices or images for data collection unless (1) the research consists solely of naturalistic observations in public places, and it is not anticipated that the recording will be used in a manner that could cause personal identification or harm, or (2) the research design includes deception, and consent for the use of the recording is obtained during debriefing. (See also Standard 8.07, Deception in Research.)

8.04 Client/Patient, Student, and Subordinate Research Participants

(a) When psychologists conduct research with clients/patients, students, or subordinates as participants, psychologists take steps to protect the prospective participants from adverse consequences of declining or withdrawing from participation.

(b) When research participation is a course requirement or an opportunity for extra credit, the prospective participant is given the choice of equitable alternative activities.

8.05 Dispensing With Informed Consent for Research

Psychologists may dispense with informed consent only (1) where research would not reasonably be assumed to create distress or harm and involves (a) the study of normal educational practices, curricula, or classroom management methods conducted in educational settings; (b) only anonymous questionnaires, naturalistic observations, or archival research for which disclosure of responses would not place participants at risk of criminal or civil liability or damage their financial standing, employability, or reputation, and confidentiality is protected; or (c) the study of factors related to job or organization effectiveness conducted in organizational settings for which there is no risk to participants' employability, and confidentiality is protected or (2) where otherwise permitted by law or federal or institutional regulations.

8.06 Offering Inducements for Research Participation

(a) Psychologists make reasonable efforts to avoid offering excessive or inappropriate financial or other inducements for research participation when such inducements are likely to coerce participation.

(b) When offering professional services as an inducement for research participation, psychologists clarify the nature of the services, as well as the risks, obligations, and limitations. (See also Standard 6.05, Barter With Clients/Patients.)

8.07 Deception in Research

(a) Psychologists do not conduct a study involving deception unless they have determined that the use of deceptive techniques is justified by the study's significant prospective scientific, educational, or applied value and that effective nondeceptive alternative procedures are not feasible.

(b) Psychologists do not deceive prospective participants about research that is reasonably expected to cause physical pain or severe emotional distress.

(c) Psychologists explain any deception that is an integral feature of the design and conduct of an experiment to participants as early as is feasible, preferably at the conclusion of their participation, but no later than at the conclusion of

the data collection, and permit participants to withdraw their data. (See also Standard 8.08, Debriefing.)

8.08 Debriefing

(a) Psychologists provide a prompt opportunity for participants to obtain appropriate information about the nature, results, and conclusions of the research, and they take reasonable steps to correct any misconceptions that participants may have of which the psychologists are aware.

(b) If scientific or humane values justify delaying or withholding this information, psychologists take reasonable measures to reduce the risk of harm.

(c) When psychologists become aware that research procedures have harmed a participant, they take reasonable steps to minimize the harm.

8.09 Humane Care and Use of Animals in Research

(a) Psychologists acquire, care for, use, and dispose of animals in compliance with current federal, state, and local laws and regulations, and with professional standards.

(b) Psychologists trained in research methods and experienced in the care of laboratory animals supervise all procedures involving animals and are responsible for ensuring appropriate consideration of their comfort, health, and humane treatment.

(c) Psychologists ensure that all individuals under their supervision who are using animals have received instruction in research methods and in the care, maintenance, and handling of the species being used, to the extent appropriate to their role. (See also Standard 2.05, Delegation of Work to Others.)

(d) Psychologists make reasonable efforts to minimize the discomfort, infection, illness, and pain of animal subjects.

(e) Psychologists use a procedure subjecting animals to pain, stress, or privation only when an alternative procedure is unavailable and the goal is justified by its prospective scientific, educational, or applied value.

(f) Psychologists perform surgical procedures under appropriate anesthesia and follow techniques to avoid infection and minimize pain during and after surgery.

(g) When it is appropriate that an animal's life be terminated, psychologists proceed rapidly, with an effort to minimize pain and in accordance with accepted procedures.

8.10 Reporting Research Results

(a) Psychologists do not fabricate data. (See also Standard 5.01a, Avoidance of False or Deceptive Statements.)

(b) If psychologists discover significant errors in their published data, they take reasonable steps to correct such errors in a correction, retraction, erratum, or other appropriate publication means.

8.11 Plagiarism

Psychologists do not present portions of another's work or data as their own, even if the other work or data source is cited occasionally.

8.12 Publication Credit

(a) Psychologists take responsibility and credit, including authorship credit, only for work they have actually performed or to which they have substantially contributed. (See also Standard 8.12b, Publication Credit.)

(b) Principal authorship and other publication credits accurately reflect the relative scientific or professional contributions of the individuals involved, regardless of their relative status. Mere possession of an institutional position, such as department chair, does not justify authorship credit. Minor contributions to the research or to the writing for publications are acknowledged appropriately, such as in footnotes or in an introductory statement.

(c) Except under exceptional circumstances, a student is listed as principal author on any multiple-authored article that is substantially based on the student's doctoral dissertation. Faculty advisors discuss publication credit with students as early as feasible and throughout the research and publication process as appropriate. (See also Standard 8.12b, Publication Credit.)

8.13 Duplicate Publication of Data

Psychologists do not publish, as original data, data that have been previously published. This does not preclude republishing data when they are accompanied by proper acknowledgment.

8.14 Sharing Research Data for Verification

(a) After research results are published, psychologists do not withhold the data on which their conclusions are based from other competent professionals who seek to verify the substantive claims through reanalysis and who intend to use such data only for that purpose, provided that the confidentiality of the participants can be protected and unless legal rights concerning proprietary data preclude their release. This does not preclude psychologists from requiring that such individuals or groups be responsible for costs associated with the provision of such information.

(b) Psychologists who request data from other psychologists to verify the substantive claims through reanalysis may use shared data only for the declared purpose. Requesting psychologists obtain prior written agreement for all other uses of the data.

8.15 Reviewers

Psychologists who review material submitted for presentation, publication, grant, or research proposal review

respect the confidentiality of and the proprietary rights in such information of those who submitted it.

9. Assessment

9.01 Bases for Assessments

(a) Psychologists base the opinions contained in their recommendations, reports, and diagnostic or evaluative statements, including forensic testimony, on information and techniques sufficient to substantiate their findings. (See also Standard 2.04, Bases for Scientific and Professional Judgments.)

(b) Except as noted in 9.01c, psychologists provide opinions of the psychological characteristics of individuals only after they have conducted an examination of the individuals adequate to support their statements or conclusions. When, despite reasonable efforts, such an examination is not practical, psychologists document the efforts they made and the result of those efforts, clarify the probable impact of their limited information on the reliability and validity of their opinions, and appropriately limit the nature and extent of their conclusions or recommendations. (See also Standards 2.01, Boundaries of Competence, and 9.06, Interpreting Assessment Results.)

(c) When psychologists conduct a record review or provide consultation or supervision and an individual examination is not warranted or necessary for the opinion, psychologists explain this and the sources of information on which they based their conclusions and recommendations.

9.02 Use of Assessments

(a) Psychologists administer, adapt, score, interpret, or use assessment techniques, interviews, tests, or instruments in a manner and for purposes that are appropriate in light of the research on or evidence of the usefulness and proper application of the techniques.

(b) Psychologists use assessment instruments whose validity and reliability have been established for use with members of the population tested. When such validity or reliability has not been established, psychologists describe the strengths and limitations of test results and interpretation.

(c) Psychologists use assessment methods that are appropriate to an individual's language preference and competence, unless the use of an alternative language is relevant to the assessment issues.

9.03 Informed Consent in Assessments

(a) Psychologists obtain informed consent for assessments, evaluations, or diagnostic services, as described in Standard 3.10, Informed Consent, except when (1) testing is mandated by law or governmental regulations; (2) informed consent is implied because testing is conducted as a routine educational, institutional, or organizational activity (e.g., when participants voluntarily agree to assessment when applying for a job); or (3) one purpose of the testing is to evaluate decisional capacity. Informed consent includes an explanation of the nature and purpose of the assessment, fees, involvement of third parties, and limits of confidentiality and sufficient opportunity for the client/patient to ask questions and receive answers.

(b) Psychologists inform persons with questionable capacity to consent or for whom testing is mandated by law or governmental regulations about the nature and purpose of the proposed assessment services, using language that is reasonably understandable to the person being assessed.

(c) Psychologists using the services of an interpreter obtain informed consent from the client/patient to use that interpreter, ensure that confidentiality of test results and test security are maintained, and include in their recommendations, reports, and diagnostic or evaluative statements, including forensic testimony, discussion of any limitations on the data obtained. (See also Standards 2.05, Delegation of Work to Others; 4.01, Maintaining Confidentiality; 9.01, Bases for Assessments; 9.06, Interpreting Assessment Results; and 9.07, Assessment by Unqualified Persons.)

9.04 Release of Test Data

(a) The term *test data* refers to raw and scaled scores, client/patient responses to test questions or stimuli, and psychologists' notes and recordings concerning client/patient statements and behavior during an examination. Those portions of test materials that include client/patient responses are included in the definition of *test data*. Pursuant to a client/patient release, psychologists provide test data to the client/patient or other persons identified in the release. Psychologists may refrain from releasing test data to protect a client/patient or others from substantial harm or misuse or misrepresentation of the data or the test, recognizing that in many instances release of confidential information under these circumstances is regulated by law. (See also Standard 9.11, Maintaining Test Security.)

(b) In the absence of a client/patient release, psychologists provide test data only as required by law or court order.

9.05 Test Construction

Psychologists who develop tests and other assessment techniques use appropriate psychometric procedures and current scientific or professional knowledge for test design, standardization, validation, reduction or elimination of bias, and recommendations for use.

9.06 Interpreting Assessment Results

When interpreting assessment results, including automated interpretations, psychologists take into account the purpose of the assessment as well as the various test factors, test-taking abilities, and other characteristics of the person being assessed, such as situational, personal, linguistic, and cultural differences, that might affect psychologists' judgments or reduce the accuracy of their interpretations. They indicate any significant limitations of

their interpretations. (See also Standards 2.01b and c, Boundaries of Competence, and 3.01, Unfair Discrimination.)

9.07 Assessment by Unqualified Persons

Psychologists do not promote the use of psychological assessment techniques by unqualified persons, except when such use is conducted for training purposes with appropriate supervision. (See also Standard 2.05, Delegation of Work to Others.)

9.08 Obsolete Tests and Outdated Test Results

(a) Psychologists do not base their assessment or intervention decisions or recommendations on data or test results that are outdated for the current purpose.

(b) Psychologists do not base such decisions or recommendations on tests and measures that are obsolete and not useful for the current purpose.

9.09 Test Scoring and Interpretation Services

(a) Psychologists who offer assessment or scoring services to other professionals accurately describe the purpose, norms, validity, reliability, and applications of the procedures and any special qualifications applicable to their use.

(b) Psychologists select scoring and interpretation services (including automated services) on the basis of evidence of the validity of the program and procedures as well as on other appropriate considerations. (See also Standard 2.01b and c, Boundaries of Competence.)

(c) Psychologists retain responsibility for the appropriate application, interpretation, and use of assessment instruments, whether they score and interpret such tests themselves or use automated or other services.

9.10 Explaining Assessment Results

Regardless of whether the scoring and interpretation are done by psychologists, by employees or assistants, or by automated or other outside services, psychologists take reasonable steps to ensure that explanations of results are given to the individual or designated representative unless the nature of the relationship precludes provision of an explanation of results (such as in some organizational consulting, preemployment or security screenings, and forensic evaluations), and this fact has been clearly explained to the person being assessed in advance.

9.11. Maintaining Test Security

The term *test materials* refers to manuals, instruments, protocols, and test questions or stimuli and does not include *test data* as defined in Standard 9.04, Release of Test Data. Psychologists make reasonable efforts to maintain the integrity and security of test materials and other assessment techniques consistent with law and contractual obligations, and in a manner that permits adherence to this Ethics Code.

10. Therapy

10.01 Informed Consent to Therapy

(a) When obtaining informed consent to therapy as required in Standard 3.10, Informed Consent, psychologists inform clients/patients as early as is feasible in the therapeutic relationship about the nature and anticipated course of therapy, fees, involvement of third parties, and limits of confidentiality and provide sufficient opportunity for the client/patient to ask questions and receive answers. (See also Standards 4.02, Discussing the Limits of Confidentiality, and 6.04, Fees and Financial Arrangements.)

(b) When obtaining informed consent for treatment for which generally recognized techniques and procedures have not been established, psychologists inform their clients/patients of the developing nature of the treatment, the potential risks involved, alternative treatments that may be available, and the voluntary nature of their participation. (See also Standards 2.01e, Boundaries of Competence, and 3.10, Informed Consent.)

(c) When the therapist is a trainee and the legal responsibility for the treatment provided resides with the supervisor, the client/patient, as part of the informed consent procedure, is informed that the therapist is in training and is being supervised and is given the name of the supervisor.

10.02 Therapy Involving Couples or Families

(a) When psychologists agree to provide services to several persons who have a relationship (such as spouses, significant others, or parents and children), they take reasonable steps to clarify at the outset (1) which of the individuals are clients/patients and (2) the relationship the psychologist will have with each person. This clarification includes the psychologist's role and the probable uses of the services provided or the information obtained. (See also Standard 4.02, Discussing the Limits of Confidentiality.)

(b) If it becomes apparent that psychologists may be called on to perform potentially conflicting roles (such as family therapist and then witness for one party in divorce proceedings), psychologists take reasonable steps to clarify and modify, or withdraw from, roles appropriately. (See also Standard 3.05c, Multiple Relationships.)

10.03 Group Therapy

When psychologists provide services to several persons in a group setting, they describe at the outset the roles and responsibilities of all parties and the limits of confidentiality.

10.04 Providing Therapy to Those Served by Others

In deciding whether to offer or provide services to those already receiving mental health services elsewhere, psychologists carefully consider the treatment issues and the potential client's/patient's welfare. Psychologists discuss these issues with the client/patient or another legally authorized person on behalf of the client/patient in order to minimize the risk of confusion and conflict, consult with the other service providers when appropriate, and proceed with caution and sensitivity to the therapeutic issues.

10.05 Sexual Intimacies With Current Therapy Clients/Patients

Psychologists do not engage in sexual intimacies with current therapy clients/patients.

10.06 Sexual Intimacies With Relatives or Significant Others of Current Therapy Clients/Patients

Psychologists do not engage in sexual intimacies with individuals they know to be close relatives, guardians, or significant others of current clients/patients. Psychologists do not terminate therapy to circumvent this standard.

10.07 Therapy With Former Sexual Partners

Psychologists do not accept as therapy clients/patients persons with whom they have engaged in sexual intimacies.

10.08 Sexual Intimacies With Former Therapy Clients/Patients

(a) Psychologists do not engage in sexual intimacies with former clients/patients for at least two years after cessation or termination of therapy.

(b) Psychologists do not engage in sexual intimacies with former clients/patients even after a two-year interval except in the most unusual circumstances. Psychologists who engage in such activity after the two years following cessation or termination of therapy and of having no sexual contact with the former client/patient bear the burden of demonstrating that there has been no exploitation, in light of all relevant factors, including (1) the amount of time that has passed since therapy terminated; (2) the nature, duration, and intensity of the therapy; (3) the circumstances of termination; (4) the client's/patient's personal history; (5) the client's/patient's current mental status; (6) the likelihood of adverse impact on the client/patient; and (7) any statements or actions made by the therapist during the course of therapy suggesting or inviting the possibility of a posttermination sexual or romantic relationship with the client/patient. (See also Standard 3.05, Multiple Relationships.)

10.09 Interruption of Therapy

When entering into employment or contractual relationships, psychologists make reasonable efforts to provide for orderly and appropriate resolution of responsibility for client/patient care in the event that the employment or contractual relationship ends, with paramount consideration given to the welfare of the client/patient. (See also Standard 3.12, Interruption of Psychological Services.)

10.10 Terminating Therapy

(a) Psychologists terminate therapy when it becomes reasonably clear that the client/patient no longer needs the service, is not likely to benefit, or is being harmed by continued service.

(b) Psychologists may terminate therapy when threatened or otherwise endangered by the client/patient or another person with whom the client/patient has a relationship.

(c) Except where precluded by the actions of clients/patients or third-party payors, prior to termination psychologists provide pretermination counseling and suggest alternative service providers as appropriate.

History and Effective Date Footnote

This version of the APA Ethics Code was adopted by the American Psychological Association's Council of Representatives during its meeting, August 21, 2002, and is effective beginning June 1, 2003. Inquiries concerning the substance or interpretation of the APA Ethics Code should be addressed to the Director, Office of Ethics, American Psychological Association, 750 First Street, NE, Washington, DC 20002-4242. The Ethics Code and information regarding the Code can be found on the APA

The APA has previously published its Ethics Code as follows:

American Psychological Association. (1953). Ethical standards of psychologists. Washington, DC: Author.

American Psychological Association. (1959). Ethical standards of psychologists. American Psychologist, 14, 279–282.

American Psychological Association. (1963). Ethical standards of psychologists. American Psychologist, 18, 56–60.

American Psychological Association. (1968). Ethical standards of psychologists. American Psychologist, 23, 357–361.

American Psychological Association. (1977, March). Ethical standards of psychologists. APA Monitor, 22–23.

American Psychological Association. (1979). Ethical standards of psychologists. Washington, DC: Author.

American Psychological Association. (1981). Ethical principles of psychologists. American Psychologist, 36, 633–638.

American Psychological Association. (1990). Ethical principles of psychologists (Amended June 2, 1989). American Psychologist, 45, 390–395.

American Psychological Association. (1992). Ethical principles of psychologists and code of conduct. American Psychologist, 47, 1597–1611.

Request copies of the APA's Ethical Principles of Psychologists and Code of Conduct from the APA Order Department, 750 First Street, NE, Washington, DC 20002-4242, or phone (202) 336–5510.

Ethics Code 2002.doc 10/8/02

CHAPTER 4

National Board for Certified Counselors Code of Ethics (2005)

The National Board for Certified Counselors (NBCC) was established in 1982 as a professional certification board to credential counselors who met standards established by the Board for the general and specialty practices of counseling. Although the Board recognizes that those who have been certified under it are diverse and licensed under jurisdictions that may have their own codes of ethics, the *NBCC Code of Ethics* provides a minimum ethical baseline for those who hold NBCC certificates. It also gives those served by NBCC providers a resource to appeal to if they perceive an ethical violation by someone who has NBCC credentials.

The *NBCC Code of Ethics* is organized into the following sections:

- General
- Counseling Relationship
- Counselor Supervision
- Measurement and Evaluation
- Research and Publication
- Consulting
- Private Practice

As with other codes of ethics, there are a number of subsections under each main section ranging in number from seventeen (17) (e.g., Counseling Relationship) to four (4) (e.g., Private Practice).

Since NBCC recognizes that those it certifies may also be governed by other professional codes of ethics, it cooperates with other professional organizations and credentialing groups when questions of ethics are raised concerning one of its certicants. Furthermore, it acts on its own to discipline or sanction those who have been found to violate the *NBCC Code of Ethics*.

NATIONAL BOARD FOR CERTIFIED COUNSELORS®
CODE OF ETHICS

PREAMBLE

The National Board for Certified Counselors (NBCC®) is a professional certification board which certifies counselors as having met standards for the general and specialty practice of professional counseling established by the Board. The counselors certified by NBCC® may identify with different professional associations and are often licensed by jurisdictions which promulgate codes of ethics. The NBCC® code of ethics provides a minimal ethical standard for the professional behavior of all NBCC® certificants. This code provides an expectation of and assurance for the ethical practice for all who use the professional services of an NBCC® certificant. In addition, it serves the purpose of having an enforceable standard for all NBCC® certificants and assures those served of some resource in case of a perceived ethical violation.

The NBCC® Ethical Code applies to all those certified by NBCC® regardless of any other professional affiliation. Persons who receive professional services from certified counselors may elect to use other ethical codes which apply to their counselor. Although NBCC® cooperates with professional associations and credentialing organizations, it can bring actions to discipline or sanction NBCC® certificants only if the provisions of the NBCC® Code are found to have been violated.

The National Board for Certified Counselors, Inc. (NBCC®) promotes counseling through certification. In pursuit of this mission, the NBCC®:

- Promotes quality assurance in counseling practice
- Promotes the value of counseling
- Promotes public awareness of quality counseling practice
- Promotes professionalism in counseling
- Promotes leadership in credentialing

Section A: General

1. Certified counselors engage in continuous efforts to improve professional practices, services, and research. Certified counselors are guided in their work by evidence of the best professional practices.

2. Certified counselors have a responsibility to the clients they serve and to the institutions within which the services are performed. Certified counselors also strive to assist the respective agency, organization, or institution in providing competent and ethical professional services. The acceptance of employment in an institution implies that the certified counselor is in agreement with the general policies and principles of the institution. Therefore, the professional activities of the certified counselor are in accord with the objectives of the institution. If the certified counselor and the employer do not agree and cannot reach agreement on policies that are consistent with appropriate counselor ethical practice that is conducive to client growth and development, the employment should be terminated. If the situation warrants further action, the certified counselor should work through professional organizations to have the unethical practice changed.

3. Ethical behavior among professional associates (i.e., both certified and non-certified counselors) must be expected at all times. When a certified counselor has doubts as to the ethical behavior of professional colleagues, the certified counselor must take action to attempt to rectify this condition. Such action uses the respective institution's channels first and then uses procedures established by the NBCC® or the perceived violator's profession.

4. Certified counselors must refuse remuneration for consultation or counseling with persons who are entitled to these services through the certified counselor's employing institution or agency. Certified counselors must not divert to their private practices, without the mutual consent of the institution and the client, legitimate clients in their primary agencies or the institutions with which they are affiliated.

5. In establishing fees for professional counseling services, certified counselors must consider the financial status of clients. In the event that the established fee status is inappropriate for a client, assistance must be provided in finding comparable services at acceptable cost.

6. Certified counselors offer only professional services for which they are trained or have supervised experience. No diagnosis, assessment, or treatment should be performed without prior training or supervision. Certified counselors are responsible for correcting any misrepresentations of their qualifications by others.

7. Certified counselors recognize their limitations and provide services or use techniques for which they are qualified by training and/or supervision. Certified counselors recognize the need for and seek continuing education to assure competent services.

8. Certified counselors are aware of the intimacy in the counseling relationship and maintain respect for the client. Counselors must not engage in activities that seek to meet their personal or professional needs at the expense of the client.

9. Certified counselors must insure that they do not engage in personal, social, organizational, financial, or political activities which might lead to a misuse of their influence.

10. Sexual intimacy with clients is unethical. Certified counselors will not be sexually, physically, or romantically intimate with clients, and they will not engage in sexual, physical, or romantic intimacy with clients within a minimum of two years after terminating the counseling relationship.

11. Certified counselors do not condone or engage in sexual harassment, which is defined as unwelcome comments, gestures, or physical contact of a sexual nature.

12. Through an awareness of the impact of stereotyping and unwarranted discrimination (e.g., biases based on age, disability, ethnicity, gender, race, religion, or sexual orientation), certified counselors guard the individual rights and personal dignity of the client in the counseling relationship.

13. Certified counselors are accountable at all times for their behavior. They must be aware that all actions and behaviors of the counselor reflect on professional integrity and, when inappropriate, can damage the public trust in the counseling profession. To protect public confidence in the counseling profession, certified counselors avoid behavior that is clearly in violation of accepted moral and legal standards.

14. Products or services provided by certified counselors by means of classroom instruction, public lectures, demonstrations, written articles, radio or television programs or other types of media must meet the criteria cited in this code.

15. Certified counselors have an obligation to withdraw from the practice of counseling if they violate the Code of Ethics, or if the mental or physical condition of the certified counselor renders it unlikely that a professional relationship will be maintained.

Section B: Counseling Relationship

1. The primary obligation of certified counselors is to respect the integrity and promote the welfare of clients, whether they are assisted individually, in family units, or in group counseling. In a group setting, the certified counselor is also responsible for taking reasonable precautions to protect individuals from physical and/or psychological trauma resulting from interaction within the group.

2. Certified counselors know and take into account the traditions and practices of other professional disciplines with whom they work and cooperate fully with such. If a person is receiving similar services from another professional, certified counselors do not offer their own services directly to such a person. If a certified counselor is contacted by a person who is already receiving similar services from another professional, the certified counselor carefully considers that professional relationship as well as the client's welfare and proceeds with caution and sensitivity to the therapeutic issues. When certified counselors learn that their clients are in a professional relationship with another counselor or mental health professional, they request release from the clients to inform the other counselor or mental health professional of their relationship with the client and strive to establish positive and collaborative professional relationships that are in the best interest of the client. Certified counselors discuss these issues with clients and the counselor or professional so as to minimize the risk of confusion and conflict and encourage clients to inform other professionals of the new professional relationship.

3. Certified counselors may choose to consult with any other professionally competent person about a client and must notify clients of this right. Certified counselors avoid placing a consultant in a conflict-of-interest situation that would preclude the consultant serving as a proper party to the efforts of the certified counselor to help the client.

4. When a client's condition indicates that there is a clear and imminent danger to the client or others, the certified counselor must take reasonable action to inform potential victims and/or inform responsible authorities. Consultation with other professionals must be used when possible. The assumption of responsibility for the client's behavior must be taken only after careful deliberation, and the client must be involved in the resumption of responsibility as quickly as possible.

5. Records of the counseling relationship, including interview notes, test data, correspondence, audio or visual tape recordings, electronic data storage, and other documents are to be considered professional information for use in counseling. Records should contain accurate factual data. The physical records are property of the certified counselors or their employers. The information contained in the records belongs to the client and therefore may not be released to others without the consent of the client or when the counselor has exhausted challenges to a court order. The certified counselors are responsible to insure that their employees handle confidential information appropriately. Confidentiality must be maintained during the storage and disposition of records. Records should be maintained for a period of at least five (5) years after the last counselor/client contact, including cases in which the client is deceased. All records must be released to the client upon request.

6. Certified counselors must ensure that data maintained in electronic storage are secure. By using the best computer security methods available, the data must be limited to information that is appropriate and necessary for the services being provided and accessible only to appropriate staff members involved in the provision of services. Certified counselors must also ensure that the electronically stored data are destroyed when the information is no longer of value in providing services or required as part of clients' records.

7. Any data derived from a client relationship and used in training or research shall be so disguised that the informed client's identity is fully protected. Any data which cannot be so disguised may be used only as expressly authorized by the client's informed and uncoerced consent.

8. When counseling is initiated, and throughout the counseling process as necessary, counselors inform clients of the purposes, goals, techniques, procedures, limitations, potential risks and benefits of services to be performed, and clearly indicate limitations that may affect the relationship as well as any other pertinent information. Counselors take reasonable steps to ensure that clients understand the implications of any diagnosis, the intended use of tests and reports, methods of treatment and safety precautions that must be taken in their use, fees, and billing arrangements.

9. Certified counselors who have an administrative, supervisory and/or evaluative relationship with individuals seeking counseling services must not serve as the counselor and should refer the individuals to other professionals. Exceptions are made only in instances where an individual's situation warrants counseling intervention and another alternative is unavailable. Dual relationships that might impair the certified counselor's objectivity and professional judgment must be avoided and/or the counseling relationship terminated through referral to a competent professional.

10. When certified counselors determine an inability to be of professional assistance to a potential or existing client, they must, respectively, not initiate the counseling relationship or immediately terminate the relationship. In either event, the certified counselor must suggest appropriate alternatives. Certified counselors must be knowledgeable about referral resources so that a satisfactory referral can be initiated. In the event that the client declines a suggested referral, the certified counselor is not obligated to continue the relationship.

11. When certified counselors are engaged in intensive, short-term counseling, they must ensure that professional assistance is available at normal costs to clients during and following the short-term counseling.

12. Counselors using electronic means in which counselor and client are not in immediate proximity must present clients with local sources of care before establishing a continued short or long-term relationship. Counselors who communicate with clients via Internet are governed by NBCC® standards for Web Counseling.

13. Counselors must document permission to practice counseling by electronic means in all governmental jurisdictions where such counseling takes place.

14. When electronic data and systems are used as a component of counseling services, certified counselors must ensure that the computer application, and any information it contains, is appropriate for the respective needs of clients and is non-discriminatory. Certified counselors must ensure that they themselves have acquired a facilitation level of knowledge with any system they use including hands-on application, and understanding of the uses of all aspects of the computer-based system. In selecting and/or maintaining computer-based systems that contain career information, counselors must ensure that the system provides current, accurate, and locally relevant information. Certified counselors must also ensure that clients are intellectually, emotionally, and physically compatible with computer applications and understand their purpose and operation. Client use of a computer application must be evaluated to correct possible problems and assess subsequent needs.

15. Certified counselors who develop self-help/stand-alone computer software for use by the general public, must first ensure that it is designed to function in a stand-alone manner that is appropriate and safe for all clients for which it is intended. A manual is required. The manual must provide the user with intended outcomes, suggestions for using the software, descriptions of inappropriately used applications, and descriptions of when and how other forms of counseling services might be beneficial. Finally, the manual must include the qualifications of the developer, the development process, validation date, and operating procedures.

16. The counseling relationship and information resulting from it remains confidential, consistent with the legal and ethical obligations of certified counselors. In group counseling, counselors clearly define confidentiality and the parameters for the specific group being entered, explain the importance of confidentiality, and discuss the difficulties related to confidentiality involved in group work. The fact that confidentiality cannot be guaranteed is clearly communicated to group members. However, counselors should give assurance about their professional responsibility to keep all group communications confidential.

17. Certified counselors must screen prospective group counseling participants to ensure compatibility with group objectives. This is especially important when the emphasis is on self-understanding and growth through self-disclosure. Certified counselors must maintain an awareness of the welfare of each participant throughout the group process.

Section C: Measurement and Evaluation

1. Because many types of assessment techniques exist, certified counselors must recognize the limits of their competence and perform only those assessment functions for which they have received appropriate training or supervision.

2. Certified counselors who utilize assessment instruments to assist them with diagnoses must have appropriate training and skills in educational and psychological meas-

urement, validation criteria, test research, and guidelines for test development and use.

3. Certified counselors must provide instrument specific orientation or information to an examinee prior to and following the administration of assessment instruments or techniques so that the results may be placed in proper perspective with other relevant factors. The purpose of testing and the explicit use of the results must be made known to an examinee prior to testing.

4. In selecting assessment instruments or techniques for use in a given situation or with a particular client, certified counselors must carefully evaluate the specific theoretical bases and characteristics, validity, reliability and appropriateness of the instrument.

5. When making statements to the public about assessment instruments or techniques, certified counselors must provide accurate information and avoid false claims or misconceptions concerning the meaning of the instrument's reliability and validity terms.

6 Counselors must follow all directions and researched procedures for selection, administration and interpretation of all evaluation instruments and use them only within proper contexts.

7. Certified counselors must be cautious when interpreting the results of instruments that possess insufficient technical data, and must explicitly state to examinees the specific limitations and purposes for the use of such instruments.

8. Certified counselors must proceed with caution when attempting to evaluate and interpret performances of any person who cannot be appropriately compared to the norms for the instrument.

9. Because prior coaching or dissemination of test materials can invalidate test results, certified counselors are professionally obligated to maintain test security.

10. Certified counselors must consider psychometric limitations when selecting and using an instrument, and must be cognizant of the limitations when interpreting the results. When tests are used to classify clients, certified counselors must ensure that periodic review and/or retesting are made to prevent client stereotyping.

11. An examinee's welfare, explicit prior understanding, and consent are the factors used when determining who receives the test results. Certified counselors must see that appropriate interpretation accompanies any release of individual or group test data (e.g., limitations of instrument and norms).

12. Certified counselors must ensure that computer-generated test administration and scoring programs function properly thereby providing clients with accurate test results.

13. Certified counselors who develop computer-based test interpretations to support the assessment process must ensure that the validity of the interpretations is established prior to the commercial distribution of the computer application.

14. Certified counselors recognize that test results may become obsolete, and avoid the misuse of obsolete data.

15. Certified counselors must not appropriate, reproduce, or modify published tests or parts thereof without acknowledgment and permission from the publisher, except as permitted by the fair educational use provisions of the U.S. copyright law.

Section D: Research and Publication

1. Certified counselors will adhere to applicable legal and professional guidelines on research with human subjects.

2. In planning research activities involving human subjects, certified counselors must be aware of and responsive to all pertinent ethical principles and ensure that the research problem, design, and execution are in full compliance with any pertinent institutional or governmental regulations.

3. The ultimate responsibility for ethical research lies with the principal researcher, although others involved in the research activities are ethically obligated and responsible for their own actions.

4. Certified counselors who conduct research with human subjects are responsible for the welfare of the subjects throughout the experiment and must take all reasonable precautions to avoid causing injurious psychological, physical, or social effects on their subjects.

5. Certified counselors who conduct research must abide by the basic elements of informed consent:

> a. fair explanation of the procedures to be followed, including an identification of those which are experimental
> b. description of the attendant discomforts and risks
> c. description of the benefits to be expected
> d. disclosure of appropriate alternative procedures that would be advantageous for subjects with an offer to answer any inquiries concerning the procedures
> e. an instruction that subjects are free to withdraw their consent and to discontinue participation in the project or activity at any time

6. When reporting research results, explicit mention must be made of all the variables and conditions known to the investigator that may have affected the outcome of the study or the interpretation of the data.

7. Certified counselors who conduct and report research investigations must do so in a manner that minimizes the possibility that the results will be misleading.

8. Certified counselors are obligated to make available sufficient original research data to qualified others who may wish to replicate the study.

9. Certified counselors who supply data, aid in the research of another person, report research results, or make original data available, must take due care to disguise the identity of respective subjects in the absence of specific authorization from the subjects to do otherwise.

10. When conducting and reporting research, certified counselors must be familiar with and give recognition to previous work on the topic, must observe all copyright laws, and must follow the principles of giving full credit to those to whom credit is due.

11. Certified counselors must give due credit through joint authorship, acknowledgment, footnote statements, or other appropriate means to those who have contributed to the research and/or publication, in accordance with such contributions.

12. Certified counselors should communicate to other counselors the results of any research judged to be of professional value. Results that reflect unfavorably on institutions, programs, services, or vested interests must not be withheld.

13. Certified counselors who agree to cooperate with another individual in research and/or publication incur an obligation to cooperate as promised in terms of punctuality of performance and with full regard to the completeness and accuracy of the information required.

14. Certified counselors must not submit the same manuscript, or one essentially similar in content, for simultaneous publication consideration by two or more journals. In addition, manuscripts that have been published in whole or substantial part should not be submitted for additional publication without acknowledgment and permission from any previous publisher.

Section E: Consulting

Consultation refers to a voluntary relationship between a professional helper and a help-needing individual, group, or social unit in which the consultant is providing help to the client(s) in defining and solving a work-related problem or potential work-related problem with a client or client system.

1. Certified counselors, acting as consultants, must have a high degree of self awareness of their own values, knowledge, skills, limitations, and needs in entering a helping relationship that involves human and/or organizational change. The focus of the consulting relationship must be on the issues to be resolved and not on the person(s) presenting the problem.

2. In the consulting relationship, the certified counselor and client must understand and agree upon the problem definition, subsequent goals, and predicted consequences of interventions selected.

3. Certified counselors acting as consultants must be reasonably certain that they, or the organization represented, have the necessary competencies and resources for giving the kind of help that is needed or that may develop later, and that appropriate referral resources are available.

4. Certified counselors in a consulting relationship must encourage and cultivate client adaptability and growth toward self-direction. Certified counselors must maintain this role consistently and not become a decision maker for clients or create a future dependency on the consultant.

Section F: Private Practice

1. In advertising services as a private practitioner, certified counselors must advertise in a manner that accurately informs the public of the professional services, expertise, and techniques of counseling available.

2. Certified counselors who assume an executive leadership role in a private practice organization do not permit their names to be used in professional notices during periods of time when they are not actively engaged in the private practice of counseling unless their executive roles are clearly stated.

3. Certified counselors must make available their highest degree (described by discipline), type and level of certification and/or license, address, telephone number, office hours, type and/or description of services, and other relevant information. Listed information must not contain false, inaccurate, misleading, partial, out-of-context, or otherwise deceptive material or statements.

4. Certified counselors who are involved in a partnership/corporation with other certified counselors and/or other professionals, must clearly specify all relevant specialties of each member of the partnership or corporation.

Appendix: Certification Examination

Applicants for the NBCC® Certification Examinations must have fulfilled all current eligibility requirements, and are responsible for the accuracy and validity of all information and/or materials provided by themselves or by others for fulfillment of eligibility criteria.

Approved on July 1, 1982
Amended on February 21, 1987, January 6, 1989, and October 31, 1997

Acknowledgment

Reference documents, statements, and sources for the development of the NBCC® Code of Ethics were as follows:

The Ethical Standards of the American Counseling Association (ACA), Responsible Uses for Standardized Testing (AMECD), codes of ethics for the American Psychological Association, and the National Career Development Association, Handbook of Standards for Computer-Based Career Information Systems (ACSCI); and Guidelines for the Use of Computer-Based Career Information and Guidance Systems (ACSCI).

CHAPTER 5

American Association for Marriage and Family Therapy (AAMFT) Code of Ethics (2001)

Marriage and family counseling is an area fraught with ethical dilemmas. The reason is that in couple and family work a number of persons are usually being treated together as a system, and it is unlikely that all members of the system have the same goals. To help marital and family therapists address ethical situations, the AAMFT has developed an ethical code whose standards define professional expectations in working with this population. The code is binding on all members of the AAMFT in all membership categories, and ignorance of the standards is not considered a valid excuse for not following them. The 2001 code is more explicit regarding implicit areas formerly known as "ethical obligations," such as sexual intimacy, discrimination, and confidentiality.

The content of the *AAMFT Code of Ethics* is organized into eight (8) sections:

- Responsibility to Clients
- Confidentiality
- Professional Competence and Integrity
- Responsibility to Students and Supervisors
- Responsibility to Research Participants
- Responsibility to the Profession
- Financial Arrangements
- Advertising

Processes for filing, investigating, and resolving complaints of unethical conduct are not contained in the ethics code itself but are described in publications distributed by the AAMFT Ethics Committee, such as *User's Guide to the AAMFT Code of Ethics* (2001). In addition, the Preamble to the Code of Ethics outlines some important information including the point that someone accused of ethical misconduct cannot resign as an escape from being investigated for ethics violations. Furthermore, the Preamble states that marriage and family therapists should meet a higher standard of conduct than is required by law if such a standard is in the *AAMFT Code of Ethics*.

Reference

American Association for Marriage and Family Therapy. (2001). *User's guide to the AAMFT Code of Ethics*. Washington, DC: Author.

AAMFT CODE OF ETHICS
Effective July 1, 2001

PREAMBLE

The Board of Directors of the American Association for Marriage and Family Therapy (AAMFT) hereby promulgates, pursuant to Article 2, Section 2.013 of the Association's Bylaws, the Revised AAMFT Code of Ethics, effective July 1, 2001.

The AAMFT strives to honor the public trust in marriage and family therapists by setting standards for ethical practice as described in this Code. The ethical standards define professional expectations and are enforced by the AAMFT Ethics Committee. The absence of an explicit reference to a specific behavior or situation in the Code does not mean that the behavior is ethical or unethical. The standards are not exhaustive. Marriage and family therapists who are uncertain about the ethics of a particular course of action are encouraged to seek counsel from consultants, attorneys, supervisors, colleagues, or other appropriate authorities.

Both law and ethics govern the practice of marriage and family therapy. When making decisions regarding professional behavior, marriage and family therapists must consider the AAMFT Code of Ethics and applicable laws and regulations. If the AAMFT Code of Ethics prescribes a standard higher than that required by law, marriage and family therapists must meet the higher standard of the AAMFT Code of Ethics. Marriage and family therapists comply with the mandates of law, but make known their commitment to the AAMFT Code of Ethics and take steps to resolve the conflict in a responsible manner. The AAMFT supports legal mandates for reporting of alleged unethical conduct.

The AAMFT Code of Ethics is binding on Members of AAMFT in all membership categories, AAMFT-Approved Supervisors, and applicants for membership and the Approved Supervisor designation (hereafter, AAMFT Member). AAMFT members have an obligation to be familiar with the AAMFT Code of Ethics and its application to their professional services. Lack of awareness or misunderstanding of an ethical standard is not a defense to a charge of unethical conduct.

The process for filing, investigating, and resolving complaints of unethical conduct is described in the current Procedures for Handling Ethical Matters of the AAMFT Ethics Committee. Persons accused are considered innocent by the Ethics Committee until proven guilty, except as otherwise provided, and are entitled to due process. If an AAMFT Member resigns in anticipation of, or during the course of, an ethics investigation, the Ethics Committee will complete its investigation. Any publication of action taken by the Association will include the fact that the Member attempted to resign during the investigation.

Contents

Principle I: Responsibility to Clients

Marriage and family therapists advance the welfare of families and individuals. They respect the rights of those persons seeking their assistance, and make reasonable efforts to ensure that their services are used appropriately.

1.1. Marriage and family therapists provide professional assistance to persons without discrimination on the basis of race, age, ethnicity, socioeconomic status, disability, gender, health status, religion, national origin, or sexual orientation.

1.2 Marriage and family therapists obtain appropriate informed consent to therapy or related procedures as early as feasible in the therapeutic relationship, and use language that is reasonably understandable to clients. The content of informed consent may vary depending upon the client and treatment plan; however, informed consent generally necessitates that the client: (a) has the capacity to consent; (b) has been adequately informed of significant information concerning treatment processes and procedures; (c) has been adequately informed of potential risks and benefits of treatments for which generally recognized standards do not yet exist; (d) has freely and without undue influence expressed consent; and (e) has provided consent that is appropriately documented. When persons, due to age or mental status, are legally incapable of giving informed consent, marriage and family therapists obtain informed permission from a legally authorized person, if such substitute consent is legally permissible.

1.3 Marriage and family therapists are aware of their influential positions with respect to clients, and they avoid exploiting the trust and dependency of such persons. Therapists, therefore, make every effort to avoid conditions and multiple relationships with clients that could impair professional judgment or increase the risk of exploitation. Such relationships include, but are not limited to, business or close personal relationships with a client or the client's immediate family. When the risk of impairment or exploitation exists due to conditions or multiple roles, therapists take appropriate precautions.

1.4 Sexual intimacy with clients is prohibited.

1.5 Sexual intimacy with former clients is likely to be harmful and is therefore prohibited for two years following the termination of therapy or last professional contact. In an effort to avoid exploiting the trust and dependency of clients, marriage and family therapists should not engage in sexual intimacy with former clients after the two years following termination or last professional contact. Should therapists engage in sexual intimacy with former clients following two years after termination or last professional contact, the burden shifts to the therapist to demonstrate that there has been no exploitation or injury to the former client or to the client's immediate family.

1.6 Marriage and family therapists comply with applicable laws regarding the reporting of alleged unethical conduct.

1.7 Marriage and family therapists do not use their professional relationships with clients to further their own interests.

1.8 Marriage and family therapists respect the rights of clients to make decisions and help them to understand the consequences of these decisions. Therapists clearly advise the clients that they have the responsibility to make decisions regarding relationships such as cohabitation, marriage, divorce, separation, reconciliation, custody, and visitation.

1.9 Marriage and family therapists continue therapeutic relationships only so long as it is reasonably clear that clients are benefiting from the relationship.

1.10 Marriage and family therapists assist persons in obtaining other therapeutic services if the therapist is unable or unwilling, for appropriate reasons, to provide professional help.

1.11 Marriage and family therapists do not abandon or neglect clients in treatment without making reasonable arrangements for the continuation of such treatment.

1.12 Marriage and family therapists obtain written informed consent from clients before videotaping, audio recording, or permitting third-party observation.

1.13 Marriage and family therapists, upon agreeing to provide services to a person or entity at the request of a third party, clarify, to the extent feasible and at the outset of the service, the nature of the relationship with each party and the limits of confidentiality.

Principle II: Confidentiality

Marriage and family therapists have unique confidentiality concerns because the client in a therapeutic relationship may be more than one person. Therapists respect and guard the confidences of each individual client.

2.1 Marriage and family therapists disclose to clients and other interested parties, as early as feasible in their professional contacts, the nature of confidentiality and possible limitations of the clients' right to confidentiality. Therapists review with clients the circumstances where confidential information may be requested and where disclosure of confidential information may be legally required. Circumstances may necessitate repeated disclosures.

2.2 Marriage and family therapists do not disclose client confidences except by written authorization or waiver, or where mandated or permitted by law. Verbal authorization will not be sufficient except in emergency situations, unless prohibited by law. When providing couple, family or group treatment, the therapist does not disclose information outside the treatment context without a written authorization from each individual competent to execute a waiver. In the context of couple, family or group treatment, the therapist may not reveal any individual's confidences to others in the client unit without the prior written permission of that individual.

2.3 Marriage and family therapists use client and/or clinical materials in teaching, writing, consulting, research, and public presentations only if a written waiver has been obtained in accordance with Subprinciple 2.2, or when appropriate steps have been taken to protect client identity and confidentiality.

2.4 Marriage and family therapists store, safeguard, and dispose of client records in ways that maintain confidentiality and in accord with applicable laws and professional standards.

2.5 Subsequent to the therapist moving from the area, closing the practice, or upon the death of the therapist, a marriage and family therapist arranges for the storage, transfer, or disposal of client records in ways that maintain confidentiality and safeguard the welfare of clients.

2.6 Marriage and family therapists, when consulting with colleagues or referral sources, do not share confidential information that could reasonably lead to the identification of a client, research participant, supervisee, or other person with whom they have a confidential relationship unless they have obtained the prior written consent of the client, research participant, supervisee, or other person with whom they have a confidential relationship. Information may be shared only to the extent necessary to achieve the purposes of the consultation.

Principle III: Professional Competence and Integrity

Marriage and family therapists maintain high standards of professional competence and integrity.

3.1 Marriage and family therapists pursue knowledge of new developments and maintain competence in marriage and family therapy through education, training, or supervised experience.

3.2 Marriage and family therapists maintain adequate knowledge of and adhere to applicable laws, ethics, and professional standards.

3.3 Marriage and family therapists seek appropriate professional assistance for their personal problems or conflicts that may impair work performance or clinical judgment.

3.4 Marriage and family therapists do not provide services that create a conflict of interest that may impair work performance or clinical judgment.

3.5 Marriage and family therapists, as presenters, teachers, supervisors, consultants and researchers, are dedicated to high standards of scholarship, present accurate information, and disclose potential conflicts of interest.

3.6 Marriage and family therapists maintain accurate and adequate clinical and financial records.

3.7 While developing new skills in specialty areas, marriage and family therapists take steps to ensure the competence of their work and to protect clients from possible harm. Marriage and family therapists practice in specialty areas new to them only after appropriate education, training, or supervised experience.

3.8 Marriage and family therapists do not engage in sexual or other forms of harassment of clients, students, trainees, supervisees, employees, colleagues, or research subjects.

3.9 Marriage and family therapists do not engage in the exploitation of clients, students, trainees, supervisees, employees, colleagues, or research subjects.

3.10 Marriage and family therapists do not give to or receive from clients (a) gifts of substantial value or (b) gifts that impair the integrity or efficacy of the therapeutic relationship.

3.11 Marriage and family therapists do not diagnose, treat, or advise on problems outside the recognized boundaries of their competencies.

3.12 Marriage and family therapists make efforts to prevent the distortion or misuse of their clinical and research findings.

3.13 Marriage and family therapists, because of their ability to influence and alter the lives of others, exercise special care when making public their professional recommendations and opinions through testimony or other public statements.

3.14 To avoid a conflict of interests, marriage and family therapists who treat minors or adults involved in custody or visitation actions may not also perform forensic evaluations for custody, residence, or visitation of the minor. The marriage and family therapist who treats the minor may provide the court or mental health professional performing the evaluation with information about the minor from the marriage and family therapist's perspective as a treating marriage and family therapist, so long as the marriage and family therapist does not violate confidentiality.

3.15 Marriage and family therapists are in violation of this Code and subject to termination of membership or other appropriate action if they: (a) are convicted of any felony; (b) are convicted of a misdemeanor related to their qualifications or functions; (c) engage in conduct which could lead to conviction of a felony, or a misdemeanor related to their qualifications or functions; (d) are expelled from or disciplined by other professional organizations; (e) have their licenses or certificates suspended or revoked or are otherwise disciplined by regulatory bodies; (f) continue to practice marriage and family therapy while no longer competent to do so because they are impaired by physical or mental causes or the abuse of alcohol or other substances; or (g) fail to cooperate with the Association at any point from the inception of an ethical complaint through the completion of all proceedings regarding that complaint.

Principle IV: Responsibility to Students and Supervisees

Marriage and family therapists do not exploit the trust and dependency of students and supervisees.

4.1 Marriage and family therapists are aware of their influential positions with respect to students and supervisees, and they avoid exploiting the trust and dependency of such persons. Therapists, therefore, make every effort to avoid conditions and multiple relationships that could impair professional objectivity or increase the risk of exploitation. When the risk of impairment or exploitation exists due to conditions or multiple roles, therapists take appropriate precautions.

4.2 Marriage and family therapists do not provide therapy to current students or supervisees.

4.3 Marriage and family therapists do not engage in sexual intimacy with students or supervisees during the evaluative or training relationship between the therapist and student or supervisee. Should a supervisor engage in sexual activity with a former supervisee, the burden of proof shifts to the supervisor to demonstrate that there has been no exploitation or injury to the supervisee.

4.4 Marriage and family therapists do not permit students or supervisees to perform or to hold themselves out as competent to perform professional services beyond their training, level of experience, and competence.

4.5 Marriage and family therapists take reasonable measures to ensure that services provided by supervisees are professional.

4.6 Marriage and family therapists avoid accepting as supervisees or students those individuals with whom a prior or existing relationship could compromise the therapist's objectivity. When such situations cannot be avoided, therapists take appropriate precautions to maintain objectivity. Examples of such relationships include, but are not limited to, those individuals with whom the therapist has a current or prior sexual, close personal, immediate familial, or therapeutic relationship.

4.7 Marriage and family therapists do not disclose supervisee confidences except by written authorization or waiver, or when mandated or permitted by law. In educational or training settings where there are multiple supervisors, disclosures are permitted only to other professional colleagues, administrators, or employers who share responsibility for training of the supervisee. Verbal authorization will not be sufficient except in emergency situations, unless prohibited by law.

Principle V: Responsibility to Research Participants

Investigators respect the dignity and protect the welfare of research participants, and are aware of applicable laws and regulations and professional standards governing the conduct of research.

5.1 Investigators are responsible for making careful examinations of ethical acceptability in planning studies. To the extent that services to research participants may be compromised by participation in research, investigators seek the ethical advice of qualified professionals not directly involved in the investigation and observe safeguards to protect the rights of research participants.

5.2 Investigators requesting participant involvement in research inform participants of the aspects of the research that might reasonably be expected to influence willingness to participate. Investigators are especially sensitive to the possibility of diminished consent when participants are also receiving clinical services, or have impairments which limit understanding and/or communication, or when participants are children.

5.3 Investigators respect each participant's freedom to decline participation in or to withdraw from a research study at any time. This obligation requires special thought

and consideration when investigators or other members of the research team are in positions of authority or influence over participants. Marriage and family therapists, therefore, make every effort to avoid multiple relationships with research participants that could impair professional judgment or increase the risk of exploitation.

5.4 Information obtained about a research participant during the course of an investigation is confidential unless there is a waiver previously obtained in writing. When the possibility exists that others, including family members, may obtain access to such information, this possibility, together with the plan for protecting confidentiality, is explained as part of the procedure for obtaining informed consent.

Principle VI: Responsibility to the Profession

Marriage and family therapists respect the rights and responsibilities of professional colleagues and participate in activities that advance the goals of the profession.

6.1 Marriage and family therapists remain accountable to the standards of the profession when acting as members or employees of organizations. If the mandates of an organization with which a marriage and family therapist is affiliated, through employment, contract or otherwise, conflict with the AAMFT Code of Ethics, marriage and family therapists make known to the organization their commitment to the AAMFT Code of Ethics and attempt to resolve the conflict in a way that allows the fullest adherence to the Code of Ethics.

6.2 Marriage and family therapists assign publication credit to those who have contributed to a publication in proportion to their contributions and in accordance with customary professional publication practices.

6.3 Marriage and family therapists do not accept or require authorship credit for a publication based on research from a student's program, unless the therapist made a substantial contribution beyond being a faculty advisor or research committee member. Coauthorship on a student thesis, dissertation, or project should be determined in accordance with principles of fairness and justice.

6.4 Marriage and family therapists who are the authors of books or other materials that are published or distributed do not plagiarize or fail to cite persons to whom credit for original ideas or work is due.

6.5 Marriage and family therapists who are the authors of books or other materials published or distributed by an organization take reasonable precautions to ensure that the organization promotes and advertises the materials accurately and factually.

6.6 Marriage and family therapists participate in activities that contribute to a better community and society, including devoting a portion of their professional activity to services for which there is little or no financial return.

6.7 Marriage and family therapists are concerned with developing laws and regulations pertaining to marriage and family therapy that serve the public interest, and with altering such laws and regulations that are not in the public interest.

6.8 Marriage and family therapists encourage public participation in the design and delivery of professional services and in the regulation of practitioners.

Principle VII: Financial Arrangements

Marriage and family therapists make financial arrangements with clients, third-party payors, and supervisees that are reasonably understandable and conform to accepted professional practices.

7.1 Marriage and family therapists do not offer or accept kickbacks, rebates, bonuses, or other remuneration for referrals; fee-for-service arrangements are not prohibited.

7.2 Prior to entering into the therapeutic or supervisory relationship, marriage and family therapists clearly disclose and explain to clients and supervisees: (a) all financial arrangements and fees related to professional services, including charges for canceled or missed appointments; (b) the use of collection agencies or legal measures for nonpayment; and (c) the procedure for obtaining payment from the client, to the extent allowed by law, if payment is denied by the third-party payor. Once services have begun, therapists provide reasonable notice of any changes in fees or other charges.

7.3 Marriage and family therapists give reasonable notice to clients with unpaid balances of their intent to seek collection by agency or legal recourse. When such action is taken, therapists will not disclose clinical information.

7.4 Marriage and family therapists represent facts truthfully to clients, third-party payors, and supervisees regarding services rendered.

7.5 Marriage and family therapists ordinarily refrain from accepting goods and services from clients in return for services rendered. Bartering for professional services may be conducted only if: (a) the supervisee or client requests it, (b) the relationship is not exploitative, (c) the professional relationship is not distorted, and (d) a clear written contract is established.

7.6 Marriage and family therapists may not withhold records under their immediate control that are requested and needed for a client's treatment solely because payment has not been received for past services, except as otherwise provided by law.

Principle VIII: Advertising

Marriage and family therapists engage in appropriate informational activities, including those that enable the public, referral sources, or others to choose professional services on an informed basis.

8.1 Marriage and family therapists accurately represent their competencies, education, training, and experience relevant to their practice of marriage and family therapy.

8.2 Marriage and family therapists ensure that advertisements and publications in any media (such as directories, announcements, business cards, newspapers, radio, television, Internet, and facsimiles) convey information that is necessary for the public to make an appropriate selection of professional services. Information could include: (a) office information, such as name, address, telephone number, credit card acceptability, fees, languages spoken, and office hours; (b) qualifying clinical degree (see subprinciple 8.5); (c) other earned degrees (see subprinciple 8.5) and state or provincial licensures and/or certifications; (d) AAMFT clinical member status; and (e) description of practice.

8.3 Marriage and family therapists do not use names that could mislead the public concerning the identity, responsibility, source, and status of those practicing under that name, and do not hold themselves out as being partners or associates of a firm if they are not.

8.4 Marriage and family therapists do not use any professional identification (such as a business card, office sign, letterhead, Internet, or telephone or association directory listing) if it includes a statement or claim that is false, fraudulent, misleading, or deceptive.

8.5 In representing their educational qualifications, marriage and family therapists list and claim as evidence only those earned degrees: (a) from institutions accredited by regional accreditation sources recognized by the United States Department of Education, (b) from institutions recognized by states or provinces that license or certify marriage and family therapists, or (c) from equivalent foreign institutions.

8.6 Marriage and family therapists correct, wherever possible, false, misleading, or inaccurate information and representations made by others concerning the therapist's qualifications, services, or products.

8.7 Marriage and family therapists make certain that the qualifications of their employees or supervisees are represented in a manner that is not false, misleading, or deceptive.

8.8 Marriage and family therapists do not represent themselves as providing specialized services unless they have the appropriate education, training, or supervised experience.

This Code is published by:
American Association for Marriage and Family Therapy
112 South Alfred Street, Alexandria, VA 22314
Phone: (703) 838-9808
Fax: (703) 838-9805
www.aamft.org

CHAPTER 6

Ethical Standards for School Counselors (2004)

School counselors and counselors who work in schools should become familiar with the *Ethical Standards for School Counselors*. This document clarifies the nature of ethical responsibilities that school counselors have and provides a benchmark for self-appraisal and peer evaluation regarding counselor responsibilities.   Specifically, it outlines school counselors' ethical obligations to the groups with whom they work.

The ASCA Ethical Standards is divided into eight (8) sections following a Preamble. The sections of the ASCA *Ethical Standards* discuss logical areas where school counselors work and have responsibilities. These areas are:

- Responsibilities to Students
- Responsibilities to Parents/Guardians
- Responsibilities to Colleagues and Professional Associates
- Responsibilities to the School and Community
- Responsibilities to the Profession
- Maintenance of Standards

Ethical Standards for School Counselors (2004)

ASCA's Ethical Standards for School Counselors were adopted by the ASCA Delegate Assembly, March 19, 1984, revised March 27, 1992, June 25, 1998 and June 26, 2004.

PREAMBLE

The American School Counselor Association (ASCA) is a professional organization whose members are certified/licensed in school counseling with unique qualifications and skills to address the academic, personal/social and career development needs of all students. Professional school counselors are advocates, leaders, collaborators and consultants who create opportunities for equity in access and success in educational opportunities by connecting their programs to the mission of schools and subscribing to the following tenets of professional responsibility:

- Each person has the right to be respected, be treated with dignity and have access to a comprehensive school counseling program that advocates for and affirms all students from diverse populations regardless of ethnic/racial status, age, economic status, special needs, English as a second language or other language group, immigration status, sexual orientation, gender, gender identity/expression, family type, religious/spiritual identity and appearance.

- Each person has the right to receive the information and support needed to move toward self-direction and self-development and affirmation within one's group identities, with special care being given to students who have historically not received adequate educational services: students of color, low socioeconomic students, students with disabilities and students with nondominant language backgrounds.

- Each person has the right to understand the full magnitude and meaning of his/her educational choices and how those choices will affect future opportunities.

- Each person has the right to privacy and thereby the right to expect the counselor–student relationship to comply with all laws, policies and ethical standards pertaining to confidentiality in the school setting.

In this document, ASCA specifies the principles of ethical behavior necessary to maintain the high standards of integrity, leadership and professionalism among its members. The Ethical Standards for School Counselors were developed to clarify the nature of ethical responsibilities held in common by school counseling professionals. The purposes of this document are to:

- Serve as a guide for the ethical practices of all professional school counselors regardless of level, area, population served or membership in this professional association;

- Provide self-appraisal and peer evaluations regarding counselor responsibilities to students, parents/guardians, colleagues and professional associates, schools, communities and the counseling profession; and

- Inform those served by the school counselor of acceptable counselor practices and expected professional behavior.

A.1. Responsibilities to Students

The professional school counselor:

a. Has a primary obligation to the student, who is to be treated with respect as a unique individual.

b. Is concerned with the educational, academic, career, personal and social needs and encourages the maximum development of every student.

c. Respects the student's values and beliefs and does not impose the counselor's personal values.

d. Is knowledgeable of laws, regulations and policies relating to students and strives to protect and inform students regarding their rights.

A.2. Confidentiality

The professional school counselor:

a. Informs students of the purposes, goals, techniques and rules of procedure under which they may receive counseling at or before the time when the counseling relationship is entered. Disclosure notice includes the limits of confidentiality such as the possible necessity for consulting with other professionals, privileged communication, and legal or authoritative restraints. The meaning and limits of confidentiality are defined in developmentally appropriate terms to students.

b. Keeps information confidential unless disclosure is required to prevent clear and imminent danger to the student or others or when legal requirements demand that confidential information be revealed. Counselors will consult with appropriate professionals when in doubt as to the validity of an exception.

c. In absence of state legislation expressly forbidding disclosure, considers the ethical responsibility to provide information to an identified third party who, by his/her relationship with the student, is at a high risk of contracting a disease that is commonly known to be communicable and fatal. Disclosure requires satisfaction of all of the following conditions:

- Student identifies partner or the partner is highly identifiable

- Counselor recommends the student notify partner and refrain from further high-risk behavior

- Student refuses

- Counselor informs the student of the intent to notify the partner

- Counselor seeks legal consultation as to the legalities of informing the partner

d. Requests of the court that disclosure not be required when the release of confidential information may potentially harm a student or the counseling relationship.

e. Protects the confidentiality of students' records and releases personal data in accordance with prescribed laws and school policies. Student information stored and transmitted electronically is treated with the same care as traditional student records.

f. Protects the confidentiality of information received in the counseling relationship as specified by federal and state laws, written policies and applicable ethical standards. Such information is only to be revealed to others with the informed consent of the student, consistent with the counselor's ethical obligation.

g. Recognizes his/her primary obligation for confidentiality is to the student but balances that obligation with an understanding of the legal and inherent rights of parents/guardians to be the guiding voice in their children's lives.

A.3. Counseling Plans

The professional school counselor:

a. Provides students with a comprehensive school counseling program that includes a strong emphasis on working jointly with all students to develop academic and career goals.

b. Advocates for counseling plans supporting students' right to choose from the wide array of options when they leave secondary education. Such plans will be regularly reviewed to update students regarding critical information they need to make informed decisions.

A.4. Dual Relationships

The professional school counselor:

a. Avoids dual relationships that might impair his/her objectivity and increase the risk of harm to the student (e.g., counseling one's family members, close friends or associates). If a dual relationship is unavoidable, the counselor is responsible for taking action to eliminate or reduce the potential for harm. Such safeguards might include informed consent, consultation, supervision and documentation.

b. Avoids dual relationships with school personnel that might infringe on the integrity of the counselor/student relationship.

A.5. Appropriate Referrals

The professional school counselor:

a. Make referrals when necessary or appropriate to outside resources. Appropriate referrals may necessitate informing both parents/guardians and students of applicable resources and making proper plans for transitions with minimal interruption of services. Students retain the right to discontinue the counseling relationship at any time.

A.6. Group Work

The professional school counselor:

a. Screens prospective group members and maintains an awareness of participants' needs and goals in relation to the goals of the group. The counselor takes reasonable precautions to protect members from physical and psychological harm resulting from interaction within the group.

b. Notifies parents/guardians and staff of group participation if the counselor deems it appropriate and if consistent with school board policy or practice.

c. Establishes clear expectations in the group setting and clearly states that confidentiality in group counseling cannot be guaranteed. Given the developmental and chronological ages of minors in schools, the counselor recognizes the tenuous nature of confidentiality for minors renders some topics inappropriate for group work in a school setting.

d. Follows up with group members and documents proceedings as appropriate.

A.7. Danger to Self or Others

The professional school counselor:

a. Informs parents/guardians or appropriate authorities when the student's condition indicates a clear and imminent danger to the student or others. This is to be done after careful deliberation and, where possible, after consultation with other counseling professionals.

b. Will attempt to minimize threat to a student and may choose to 1) inform the student of actions to be taken, 2) involve the student in a three-way communication with parents/guardians when breaching confidentiality or 3) allow the student to have input as to how and to whom the breach will be made.

A.8. Student Records

The professional school counselor:

a. Maintains and secures records necessary for rendering professional services to the student as required by laws, regulations, institutional procedures and confidentiality guidelines.

b. Keeps sole-possession records separate from students' educational records in keeping with state laws.

c. Recognizes the limits of sole-possession records and understands these records are a memory aid for the creator and in absence of privilege communication may be subpoenaed and may become educational records when they 1) are shared with others in verbal or written form, 2) include information other than professional opinion or personal observations and/or 3) are made accessible to others.

d. Establishes a reasonable timeline for purging sole-possession records or case notes. Suggested guidelines include shredding sole possession records when the student transitions to the next level, transfers to another school or graduates. Careful discretion and deliberation should be applied before destroying sole-possession records that may be needed by a court of law such as notes on child abuse, suicide, sexual harassment or violence.

A.9. Evaluation, Assessment and Interpretation

The professional school counselor:

a. Adheres to all professional standards regarding selecting, administering and interpreting assessment measures and only utilizes assessment measures that are within the scope of practice for school counselors.

b. Seeks specialized training regarding the use of electronically based testing programs in administering, scoring and interpreting that may differ from that required in more traditional assessments.

c. Considers confidentiality issues when utilizing evaluative or assessment instruments and electronically based programs.

d. Provides interpretation of the nature, purposes, results and potential impact of assessment/evaluation measures in language the student(s) can understand.

e. Monitors the use of assessment results and interpretations, and takes reasonable steps to prevent others from misusing the information.

f. Uses caution when utilizing assessment techniques, making evaluations and interpreting the performance of populations not represented in the norm group on which an instrument is standardized.

g. Assesses the effectiveness of his/her program in having an impact on students' academic, career and personal/social development through accountability measures especially examining efforts to close achievement, opportunity, and attainment gaps.

A.10. Technology

The professional school counselor:

a. Promotes the benefits of and clarifies the limitations of various appropriate technological applications. The counselor promotes technological applications (1) that are appropriate for the student's individual needs, (2) that the student understands how to use and (3) for which follow-up counseling assistance is provided.

b. Advocates for equal access to technology for all students, especially those historically underserved.

c. Takes appropriate and reasonable measures for maintaining confidentiality of student information and educational records stored or transmitted over electronic media including although not limited to fax, electronic mail, and instant messaging.

d. While working with students on a computer or similar technology, takes reasonable and appropriate measures to protect students from objectionable and/or harmful online material.

e. Who is engaged in the delivery of services involving technologies such as the telephone, videoconferencing, and the Internet, takes responsible steps to protect students and others from harm.

A.11. Student Peer Support Program

The professional school counselor:

Has unique responsibilities when working with student-assistance programs. The school counselor is responsible for the welfare of students participating in peer-to-peer programs under his/her direction.

B. RESPONSIBILITIES TO PARENTS/GUARDIANS

B.1. Parent Rights and Responsibilities

The professional school counselor:

a. Respects the rights and responsibilities of parents/guardians for their children and endeavors to establish, as appropriate, a collaborative relationship with parents/guardians to facilitate the student's maximum development.

b. Adheres to laws, local guidelines and ethical standards of practice when assisting parents/guardians experiencing family difficulties that interfere with the student's effectiveness and welfare.

c. Respects the confidentiality of parents/guardians.

d. Is sensitive to diversity among families and recognizes that all parents/guardians, custodial and noncustodial, are vested with certain rights and responsibilities for the welfare of their children by virtue of their role and according to law.

B.2. Parents/Guardians and Confidentiality

The professional school counselor:

a. Informs parents/guardians of the counselor's role with emphasis on the confidential nature of the counseling relationship between the counselor and student.

b. Recognizes that working with minors in a school setting may require counselors to collaborate with student's parents/guardians.

c. Provides parents/guardians with accurate, comprehensive and relevant information in an objective and caring manner, as is appropriate and consistent with ethical responsibilities to the student.

d. Makes reasonable efforts to honor the wishes of parents/guardians concerning information regarding the student, and in cases of divorce or separation exercises a good-faith effort to keep both parents informed with regard to critical information with the exception of a court order.

C. RESPONSIBILITIES TO COLLEAGUES AND PROFESSIONAL ASSOCIATES

C.1. Professional Relationships

The professional school counselor:

a. Establishes and maintains professional relationships with faculty, staff, and administration to facilitate an optimum counseling program.

b. Treats colleagues with professional respect, courtesy, and fairness. The qualifications, views and findings of colleagues are represented to accurately reflect the image of competent professionals.

c. Is aware of and utilizes related professionals, organizations, and other resources to whom the student may be referred.

C.2. Sharing Information with Other Professionals

The professional school counselor:

a. Promotes awareness and adherence to appropriate guidelines regarding confidentiality, the distinction between public and private information and staff consultation.

b. Provides professional personnel with accurate, objective, concise and meaningful data necessary to adequately evaluate, counsel and assist the student.

c. If a student is receiving services from another counselor or other mental health professional, the counselor, with student and/or parent/guardian consent,

will inform the other professional and develop clear agreements to avoid confusion and conflict for the student.

d. Is knowledgeable about release of information and parental rights in sharing information.

D. RESPONSIBILITIES TO THE SCHOOL AND COMMUNITY

D.1. Responsibilities to the School

The professional school counselor:

a. Supports and protects the educational program against any infringement not in students' best interest.

b. Informs appropriate officials in accordance with school policy of conditions that may be potentially disruptive or damaging to the school's mission, personnel, and property while honoring the confidentiality between the student and counselor.

c. Is knowledgeable and supportive of the school's mission and connects his/her program to the school's mission.

d. Delineates and promotes the counselor's role and function in meeting the needs of those served. Counselors will notify appropriate officials of conditions that may limit or curtail their effectiveness in providing programs and services.

e. Accepts employment only for positions for which he/she is qualified by education, training, supervised experience, state and national professional credentials and appropriate professional experience.

f. Advocates that administrators hire only qualified and competent individuals for professional counseling positions.

g. Assists in developing: (1) curricular and environmental conditions appropriate for the school and community, (2) educational procedures and programs to meet students' developmental needs, and (3) a systematic evaluation process for comprehensive, developmental, standards-based school counseling programs, services, and personnel. The counselor is guided by the findings of the evaluation data in planning programs and services.

D.2. Responsibility to the Community

The professional school counselor:

a. Collaborates with agencies, organizations, and individuals in the community in the best interest of students and without regard to personal reward or remuneration.

b. Extends his/her influence and opportunity to deliver a comprehensive school counseling program to all students by collaborating with community resources for student success.

E. RESPONSIBILITIES TO SELF

E.1. Professional Competence

The professional school counselor:

a. Functions within the boundaries of individual professional competence and accepts responsibility for the consequences of his/her actions.

b. Monitors personal well-being and effectiveness and does not participate in any activity that may lead to inadequate professional services or harm to a student.

c. Strives through personal initiative to maintain professional competence including technological literacy and to keep abreast of professional information. Professional and personal growth are ongoing throughout the counselor's career.

E.2. Diversity

The professional school counselor:

a. Affirms the diversity of students, staff, and families.

b. Expands and develops awareness of his/her own attitudes and beliefs affecting cultural values and biases and strives to attain cultural competence.

c. Possesses knowledge and understanding about how oppression, racism, discrimination, and stereotyping affects her/him personally and professionally.

d. Acquires educational, consultation and training experiences to improve awareness, knowledge, skills, and effectiveness in working with diverse populations: ethnic/racial status, age, economic status, special needs, ESL or ELL, immigration status, sexual orientation, gender, gender identity/expression, family type, religious/spiritual identity, and appearance.

F. RESPONSIBILITIES TO THE PROFESSION

F.1. Professionalism

The professional school counselor:

a. Accepts the policies and procedures for handling ethical violations as a result of maintaining membership in the American School Counselor Association.

b. Conducts herself/himself in such a manner as to advance individual ethical practice and the profession.

c. Conducts appropriate research and report findings in a manner consistent with acceptable educational and psychological research practices. The counselor advocates for the protection of the individual student's

identity when using data for research or program planning.

d. Adheres to ethical standards of the profession, other official policy statements, such as ASCA's position statements, role statement and the ASCA National Model, and relevant statutes established by federal, state and local governments, and when these are in conflict works responsibly for change.

e. Clearly distinguishes between statements and actions made as a private individual and those made as a representative of the school counseling profession.

f. Does not use his/her professional position to recruit or gain clients, consultees for his/her private practice or to seek and receive unjustified personal gains, unfair advantage, inappropriate relationships or unearned goods or services.

F.2. Contribution to the Profession

The professional school counselor:

a. Actively participates in local, state and national associations fostering the development and improvement of school counseling.

b. Contributes to the development of the profession through the sharing of skills, ideas, and expertise with colleagues.

c. Provides support and mentoring to novice professionals.

G. MAINTENANCE OF STANDARDS

Ethical behavior among professional school counselors, association members and nonmembers, is expected at all times. When there exists serious doubt as to the ethical behavior of colleagues or if counselors are forced to work in situations or abide by policies that do not reflect the standards as outlined in these Ethical Standards for School Counselors; the counselor is obligated to take appropriate action to rectify the condition. The following procedure may serve as a guide:

1. The counselor should consult confidentially with a professional colleague to discuss the nature of a complaint to see if the professional colleague views the situation as an ethical violation.

2. When feasible, the counselor should directly approach the colleague whose behavior is in question to discuss the complaint and seek resolution.

3. If resolution is not forthcoming at the personal level, the counselor shall utilize the channels established within the school, school district, the state school counseling association, and ASCA's Ethics Committee.

4. If the matter still remains unresolved, referral for review and appropriate action should be made to the Ethics Committees in the following sequence:

- state school counselor association
- American School Counselor Association

5. The ASCA Ethics Committee is responsible for:

- educating and consulting with the membership regarding ethical standards
- periodically reviewing and recommending changes in code
- receiving and processing questions to clarify the application of such standards; questions must be submitted in writing to the ASCA Ethics chair.
- handling complaints of alleged violations of the ethical standards. At the national level, complaints should be submitted in writing to the ASCA Ethics Committee, c/o the Executive Director, American School Counselor Association, 1101 King St., Suite 625, Alexandria, VA 22314.

Source: Reprinted by permission of American School Counseling Association.

CHAPTER 7

Code of Ethics of the American Mental Health Counselors Association (AMHCA) (2000)

The *Code of Ethics of the AMHCA* is based on a number of beliefs and commitments including a belief in the dignity and worth of all individuals, a belief in freedom and responsibility, a commitment to increasing knowledge of human behavior, and a commitment to the proper use of clinical skills. It is in pursuit of these ideals that the fifteen (15) principles of the code of ethics are based. These principles are listed under clinical issues and professional issues.

Under the clinical issues section of the code, there are six (6) principles:

- Welfare of the Consumer
- Clients' Rights
- Confidentiality
- Utilization of Assessment Techniques
- Pursuit of Research Activities
- Consulting

Under the professional issues section of the code, the remaining nine (9) principles fall under the following headings:

- Competence
- Professional Relationships
- Supervisee, Student and Employee Relationships
- Moral and Legal Standards
- Professional Responsibility
- Private Practice
- Public Statements
- Internet On-Line Counseling
- Resolution of Ethical Problems

As with the other codes in this guide, there are subsections under each of the principles ranging from one (1) (e.g., Public Statements) to eighteen (18) (e.g., Primary Responsibility). It is interesting to note that the *Code of Ethics of the AMHCA* covers the resolution of ethical problems within the document itself.

CODE OF ETHICS OF THE AMERICAN MENTAL HEALTH COUNSELORS ASSOCIATION
2000 Revision

PREAMBLE

Mental health counselors believe in the dignity and worth of the individual. They are committed to increasing knowledge of human behavior and understanding of themselves and others. While pursuing these endeavors, they make every reasonable effort to protect the welfare of those who seek their services, or of any subject that may be the object of study. They use their skills only for purposes consistent with these values and do not knowingly permit their misuse by others. While demanding for themselves freedom of inquiry and community, mental health counselors accept the responsibility this freedom confers: competence, objectivity in the application of skills, and concern for the best interest of clients, colleagues, and society in general.

In the pursuit of these ideals, mental health counselors subscribe to the following principles:

Principle 1 Welfare of the Consumer
Principle 2 Clients' Rights
Principle 3 Confidentiality
Principle 4 Utilization of Assessment Techniques
Principle 5 Pursuit of Research Activities
Principle 6 Consulting
Principle 7 Competence
Principle 8 Professional Relationships
Principle 9 Supervisee, Student and Employee Relationships
Principle 10 Moral and Legal Standards
Principle 11 Professional Responsibility
Principle 12 Private Practice
Principle 13 Public Statements
Principle 14 Internet On-Line Counseling
Principle 15 Resolution of Ethical Problems

Clinical Issues

Principle 1 Welfare of the Consumer

A) Primary Responsibility

1. The primary responsibility of the mental health counselor is to respect the dignity and integrity of the client. Client growth and development are encouraged in ways that foster the client's interest and promote welfare.
2. Mental health counselors are aware of their influential position with respect to their clients, and avoid exploiting the trust and fostering dependency of their clients.
3. Mental health counselors fully inform consumers as to the purpose and nature of any evaluation, treatment, education or training procedure and they fully acknowledge that the consumer has the freedom of choice with regard to participation.

B) Counseling Plans

Mental health counselors and their clients work jointly in devising integrated, individual counseling plans that offer reasonable promise of success and are consistent with the abilities and circumstances of the client. Counselors and clients regularly review counseling plans to ensure their continued viability and effectiveness, respecting the client's freedom of choice.

C) Freedom of Choice

Mental health counselors offer clients the freedom to choose whether to enter into a counseling relationship and determine which professionals will provide the counseling. Restrictions that limit clients' choices are fully explained.

D) Clients Served by Others

If a client is receiving services from another mental health professional or counselor, the mental health counselor secures consent from the client, informs that professional of the arrangement, and develops a clear agreement to avoid confusion and conflicts for the client.

1. Mental health counselors are aware of the intimacy and responsibilities inherent in the counseling relationship. They maintain respect for the client and avoid actions that seek to meet their personal needs at the expense of the client. Mental health counselors are aware of their own values, attitudes, beliefs and behaviors, and how these apply in a diverse society. They avoid imposing their values on the consumer.

E) Diversity

1. Mental health counselors do not condone or engage in any discrimination based on age, color, culture, disability, ethnic group, gender, race, religion, sexual orientation, marital status or socioeconomic status.

2. Mental health counselors will actively attempt to understand the diverse cultural backgrounds of the clients with whom they work. This includes learning how the counselor's own cultural/ethical/racial/religious identity impacts his or her own values and beliefs about the counseling process. When there is a conflict between the client's goals, identity and/or values and those of the mental health counselor, a referral to an appropriate colleague must be arranged.

F) Dual Relationships

Mental health counselors are aware of their influential position with respect to their clients and avoid exploiting the trust and fostering dependency of the client.

1. Mental health counselors make every effort to avoid dual relationships with clients that could impair professional judgement or increase the risk of harm. Examples of such relationships may include, but are not limited to: familial, social, financial, business, or close personal relationships with the clients.

2. Mental health counselors do not accept as clients individuals with whom they are involved in an administrative, supervisory, and evaluative nature. When acting as supervisors, trainers, or employers, mental health counselors accord recipients informed choice, confidentiality and protection from physical and mental harm.

3. When a dual relationship cannot be avoided, counselors take appropriate professional precautions such as informed consent, consultation, supervision and documentation to ensure that judgement is not impaired and no exploitation has occurred.

G) Sexual Relationships

Sexual relationships with clients are strictly prohibited. Mental health counselors do not counsel persons with whom they have had a previous sexual relationship.

H) Former Clients

Counselors do not engage in sexual intimacies with former clients within a minimum of two years after terminating the counseling relationship. The mental health counselor has the responsibility to examine and document thoroughly that such relations did not have an exploitative nature based on factors such as duration of counseling, amount of time since counseling, termination circumstances, the client's personal history and mental status, adverse impact on the client, and actions by the counselor suggesting a plan to initiate a sexual relationship with the client after termination.

I) Multiple Clients

When mental health counselors agree to provide counseling services to two or more persons who have a relationship (such as husband and wife, or parents and children), counselors clarify at the outset which person or persons

are clients, and the nature of the relationship they will have with each involved person. If it becomes apparent that counselors may be called upon to perform potentially conflicting roles, they clarify, adjust, or withdraw from roles appropriately.

J) Informed Consent

Mental health counselors are responsible for making their services readily accessible to clients in a manner that facilitates the clients' abilities to make an informed choice when selecting a provider. This responsibility includes a clear description of what the client can expect in the way of tests, reports, billing, therapeutic regime and schedules, and the use of the mental health counselor's statement of professional disclosure. In the event that a client is a minor or possesses disabilities that would prohibit informed consent, the mental health counselor acts in the client's best interest.

K) Conflict of Interest

Mental health counselors are aware of possible conflicts of interests that may involve the organization in which they are employed and their client. When conflicts occur, mental health counselors clarify the nature of the conflict and inform all parties of the nature and direction of their loyalties and responsibilities, and keep all parties informed of their commitments.

L) Fees and Bartering

1. Mental health counselors clearly explain to clients, prior to entering the counseling relationship, all financial arrangements related to professional services, including the use of collection agencies or legal measures for nonpayment.

2. In establishing fees for professional counseling services, mental health counselors consider the financial status of their clients and locality. In the event that the payment of the mental health counselor's usual fees would create undue hardship for the client, assistance is provided in attempting to find comparable services at an acceptable cost.

3. Mental health counselors ordinarily refrain from accepting goods or services from clients in return for counseling service because such arrangements create inherent potential for conflicts, exploitation and distortion of the professional relationship. Participation in bartering is only used when there is no exploitation, if the client requests it, if a clear written contract is established, and if such an arrangement is an accepted practice among professionals in the community.

M) Pro Bono Service

Mental health counselors contribute to society by devoting a portion of their professional activity to services for which there is little or no financial return.

N) Consulting

Mental health counselors may choose to consult with any other professionally competent person about a client. In choosing a consultant, the mental health counselor should avoid placing the consultant in a conflict of interest situation that would preclude the consultant from being a proper party to the mental health counselor's effort to help the client.

O) Group Work

1. Mental health counselors screen prospective group counseling/therapy participants. Every effort is made to select members whose needs and goals are compatible with goals of the group, who will not impede the group process, and whose well being will not be jeopardized by the group experience.

2. In the group setting, mental health counselors take reasonable precautions to protect clients from physical and psychological harm or trauma.

3. When the client is engaged in short term group treatment/training programs, i.e. marathons and other encounter type or growth groups, the members ensure that there is professional assistance available during and following the group experience.

P) Termination and Referral

Mental health counselors do not abandon or neglect their clients in counseling. Assistance is given in making appropriate arrangements for the continuation of treatment, when necessary, during interruptions such as vacation and following termination.

Q) Inability to assist clients

If the mental health counselor determines that their services are not beneficial to the client, they avoid entering or terminate immediately a counseling relationship. Mental health counselors are knowledgeable about referral sources and appropriate referrals are made. If clients decline the suggested referral, mental health counselors discontinue the relationship.

R) Appropriate Termination

Mental health counselors terminate a counseling relationship, securing a client's agreement when possible, when it is reasonably clear that the client is no longer benefiting, when services are no longer required, when counseling no longer serves the needs and interests of the client, when clients do not pay fees charged, or when agency or institution limits do not allow provision of further counseling services.

Principle 2   Clients' Rights

The following apply to all consumers of mental health services, including both in- and out-patients and all state, county, local, and private care mental health facilities, as well as clients of mental health practitioners in private practice.

The client has the right:

A) To be treated with dignity, consideration and respect at all times;

B) To expect quality service provided by concerned, trained, professional and competent staff;

C) To expect complete confidentiality within the limits of the law, and to be informed about the legal exceptions to confidentiality; and to expect that no information will be released without the client's knowledge and written consent;

D) To a clear working contract in which business items, such as time of sessions, payment plans/fees, absences, access, emergency procedures, and third-party reimbursement procedures are discussed;

E) To a clear statement of the purposes, goals, techniques, rules of procedure and limitations, as well as the potential dangers of the services to be performed, and all other information related to or likely to affect the ongoing mental health counseling relationship;

F) To appropriate information regarding the mental health counselor's education, training, skills, license and practice limitations and to request and receive referrals to other clinicians when appropriate;

G) To full, knowledgeable, and responsible participation in the ongoing treatment plan to the maximum extent feasible;

H) To obtain information about their case record and to have this information explained clearly and directly;

I) To request information and/or consultation regarding the conduct and progress of their therapy;

J) To refuse any recommended services and to be advised of the consequences of this action;

K) To a safe environment free of emotional, physical and sexual abuse;

L) To a client grievance procedure, including requests for consultation and/or mediation; and to file a complaint with the mental health counselor's supervisor, and/or the appropriate credentialing body; and

M) To a clearly defined ending process, and to discontinue therapy at any time.

Principle 3   Confidentiality

Mental health counselors have a primary obligation to safeguard information about individuals obtained in the course of practice, teaching, or research. Personal information is communicated to others only with the person's written consent or in those circumstances where there is clear and imminent danger to the client, to others or to society. Disclosure of counseling information is restricted to what is necessary, relevant and verifiable.

A) At the outset of any counseling relationship, mental health counselors make their clients aware of their rights in regard to the confidential nature of the counseling relationship. They fully disclose the limits of, or exceptions to, confidentiality, and/or the existence of privileged communication, if any.

B) All materials in the official record shall be shared with the client, who shall have the right to decide what information may be shared with anyone beyond the immediate provider of service and be informed of the implications of the materials to be shared.

C) Confidentiality belongs to the clients. They may direct the mental health counselor, in writing, to release information to others. The release of information without the consent of the client may only take place under the most extreme circumstances. The protection of life, as in the case of suicidal or homicidal clients, exceeds the requirements of confidentiality. The protection of a child, an elderly person, or a person not competent to care for themselves from physical or sexual abuse or neglect requires that a report be made to a legally constituted authority. The mental health counselor complies with all state and federal statutes concerning mandated reporting of suicidality, homicidality, child abuse, incompetent person abuse and elder abuse. The protection of the public or another individual from a contagious condition known to be fatal also requires action that may include reporting the willful infection of another with the condition.

The mental health counselor (or staff member) does not release information by request unless accompanied by a specific release of information or a valid court order. Mental health counselors will comply with the order of a court to release information but they will inform the client of the receipt of such an order. A subpoena is insufficient to release information. In such a case, the counselor must inform his client of the situation and, if the client refuses release, coordinate between the client's attorney and the requesting attorney so as to protect client confidentiality and one's own legal welfare.

In the case of all of the above exceptions to confidentiality, the mental health counselor will release only such information as is necessary to accomplish the action required by the exception.

D) The anonymity of clients served in public and other agencies is preserved, if at all possible, by withholding names and personal identifying data. If external conditions require reporting such information, the client shall be so informed.

E) Information received in confidence by one agency or person shall not be forwarded to another person or agency without the client's written permission.

F) Service providers have the responsibility to ensure the accuracy and to indicate the validity of data shared with their parties.

G) Case reports presented in classes, professional meetings, or publications shall be so disguised that no identification is possible unless the client or responsible authority has read the report and agreed in writing to its presentation or publication.

H) Counseling reports and records are maintained under conditions of security, and provisions are made for their destruction when they have outlived their usefulness. Mental health counselors ensure that all persons in his or her employ, volunteers, and community aides maintain privacy and confidentiality.

I) Mental health counselors who ask that an individual reveal personal information in the course of interviewing, testing or evaluation, or who allow such information to be divulged, do so only after making certain that the person or authorized representative is fully aware of the purposes of the interview, testing or evaluation, and of the ways in which the information will be used.

J) Sessions with clients may be taped or otherwise recorded only with their written permission or the written permission of a responsible guardian. Even with a guardian's written consent, one should not record a session against the expressed wishes of a client. Such tapes shall be destroyed when they have outlived their usefulness.

K) Where a child or adolescent is the primary client, or the client is not competent to give consent, the interests of the minor or the incompetent client shall be paramount. Where appropriate, a parent(s) or guardian(s) may be included in the counseling process. The mental health counselor must still take measures to safeguard the client's confidentiality.

L) In work with families, the rights of each family member should be safeguarded. The provider of service also has the responsibility to discuss the contents of the record with the parent and/or child, as appropriate, and to keep separate those parts, which should remain the property of each family member.

M) In work with groups, the rights of each group member should be safeguarded. The provider of service also has the responsibility to discuss the need for each member to respect the confidentiality of each other member of the group. He must also remind the group of the limits on and risk to confidentiality inherent in the group process.

N) When using a computer to store confidential information, mental health counselors take measures to control access to such information. When such information has outlived its usefulness, it should be deleted from the system.

Principle 4 Utilization of Assessment Techniques

A) Test Selection

1. In choosing a particular test, mental health counselors should ascertain that there is sufficient evidence in the test manual of its applicability in measuring a certain trait or construct. The manual should fully describe the development of the test, the rationale, and data pertaining to item selection and test construction. The manual should explicitly state the purposes and applications for which the test is intended, and provide reliability and validity data about the test. The manual should furthermore identify the qualifications necessary to properly administer and interpret the test.

2. In selecting a particular combination of tests, mental health counselors need to be able to justify the logic of those choices.

3. Mental health counselors should employ only those tests for which they judge themselves competent by training, education, or experience. In familiarizing themselves with new tests, counselors thoroughly read the manual and seek workshops, supervision, or other forms of training.

4. Mental health counselors avoid using outdated or obsolete tests, and strive to remain current regarding test publication and revision.

5. Tests selected for individual testing must be appropriate for that individual in that appropriate norms exist for variables such as age, gender, and race. The test form must fit the client. If the test must be used in the absence of available information regarding the above subsamples, the limitations of generalizability should be duly noted.

B) Test Administration

1. Mental health counselors should faithfully follow instructions for administration of a test in order to ensure standardization. Failure to consistently follow test instructions will result in test error and incorrect estimates of the trait or behavior being measured.

2. Tests should only be employed in appropriate professional settings or as recommended by instructors or supervisors for training purposes. It is best to avoid giving tests to relatives, close friends or business associates, in that doing so constructs a dual professional/personal relationship, which is to be avoided.

3. Mental health counselors should provide the test taker with appropriate information regarding the reason for assessment, the approximate length of time required, and to whom the report will be distributed. Issues of confidentiality must be addressed, and the client must be given the opportunity to ask questions of the examiner prior to beginning the procedure.

4. Care should be taken to provide an appropriate assessment environment in regard to temperature, privacy, comfort, and freedom from distractions.

5. Information should be solicited regarding any possible handicaps, such as problems with visual or auditory acuity, limitations of hand/eye coordination, illness, or other factors. If the disabilities cannot be accommodated effectively, the test may need to be postponed or the limitations of applicability of the test results noted in the test report.

6. Professionals who supervise others should ensure that their trainees have sufficient knowledge and experience before utilizing the tests for clinical purposes.

7. Mental health counselors must be able to document appropriate education, training, and experience in areas of assessment they perform.

C) Test Interpretation

1. Interpretation of test or test battery results should be based on multiple sources of convergent data and an understanding of the tests' foundations and limits.

2. Mental health counselors must be careful not to make conclusions unless empirical evidence is present to justify the statement. If such evidence is lacking, one should not make diagnostic or prognostic formulations.

3. Interpretation of test results should take into account the many qualitative influences on test-taking behavior, such as health, energy, motivation, and the like. Description and analysis of alternative explanations should be provided with the interpretations.

4. One should not make firm conclusions in the absence of published information that establishes a satisfactory degree of test validity, particularly predictive validity.

5. Multicultural factors must be considered in test interpretation and diagnosis, and formulation of prognosis and treatment recommendations.

6. Mental health counselors should avoid biased or incorrect interpretation by assuring that the test norms reference the population taking the test.

7. Mental health counselors are responsible for evaluating the quality of computer software interpretations

of test data. Mental health counselors should obtain information regarding validity of computerized test interpretation before utilizing such an approach.

8. Supervisors should ensure that their supervisees have had adequate training in interpretation before entrusting them to evaluate tests in a semi-autonomous fashion.

9. Any individual or organization offering test scoring or interpretation services must be able to demonstrate that their programs are based on sufficient and appropriate research to establish the validity of the programs and procedures used in arriving at interpretations. The public offering of an automated test interpretation service will be considered a professional-to-professional consultation. The formal responsibility of the consultant is to the consultee, but his or her ultimate and overriding responsibility is to the client.

10. Mental health counselors who have the responsibility for making decisions about clients or policies based on test results should have a thorough understanding of counseling theory, assessment techniques, and test research.

11. Mental health counselors do not represent computerized test interpretations as their own and clearly designate such computerized results.

D) Test Reporting

1. Mental health counselors should write reports in a clear fashion, avoiding excessive jargon or clinical terms that are likely to confuse the lay reader.

2. Mental health counselors should strive to provide test results in as positive and nonjudgmental manner as possible.

3. Mindful that one's report reflects on the reputation of oneself and one's profession, reports are carefully proofread so as to be free of spelling, style, and grammatical errors as much as is possible.

4. Clients should be clearly informed about who will be allowed to review the report and, in the absence of a valid court order, must sign appropriate releases of information permitting such release. Mental health counselors must not release the report or findings in the absence of the aforementioned releases or order.

5. Mental health counselors are responsible for ensuring the confidentiality and security of test reports, test data, and test materials.

6. Mental health counselors must offer the client the opportunity to receive feedback about the test results, interpretations, and the range of error for such data.

7. Transmissions of test data or test reports by fax or e-mail must be accomplished in a secure manner, with guarantees that the receiving device is capable of providing a confidential transmission only to the party who has been permitted to receive the document.

8. Mental health counselors should train his or her staff to respect the confidentiality of test reports in the context of typing, filing, or mailing them.

9. Mental health counselors (or staff members) do not release a psychological evaluation by request unless accompanied by a specific release of information or a valid court order. A subpoena is insufficient to release a report. In such a case, the counselor must inform his/her client of the situation and, if the client refuses release, coordinate between the client's attorney and the requesting attorney so as to protect client confidentiality and one's own legal welfare.

Principle 5   Pursuit of Research Activities

Mental health counselors who conduct research must do so with regard to ethical principles. The decision to undertake research should rest upon a considered judgment by the individual counselor about how best to contribute to counseling and to human welfare. Mental health counselors carry out their investigations with respect for the people who participate and with concern for their dignity and welfare.

1. The ethical researcher seeks advice from other professionals if any plan of research suggests a deviation from any ethical principle of research with human subjects. Such deviation must still protect the dignity and welfare of the client and places on the researcher a special burden to act in the subject's interest.

2. The ethical researcher is open and honest in the relationship with research participants. a) The ethical researcher informs the participant of all features of the research that might be expected to influence willingness to participate and explains to the participant all other aspects about which the participant inquires. b) Where scientific or human values justify delaying or withholding information, the investigator acquires a special responsibility to assure that there are no damaging consequences for the participants. c) Following the collection of the data, the ethical researcher must provide the participant with a full clarification of the nature of the study to remove any misconceptions that may have arisen. d) As soon as possible, the participant is to be informed of the reasons for concealment or deception that are part of the methodological requirements of a study. e) Such misinformation must be minimized and full disclosure must be made at the conclusion of all research studies. f) The ethical researcher understands that failure to make full disclo-

sure to a research participant gives added emphasis to the researcher's abiding responsibility to protect the welfare and dignity of the participant.

3. The ethical researcher protects participants from physical and mental discomfort, harm and danger. If the risks of such consequences exist, the investigator is required to inform the participant of that fact, secure consent before proceeding, and take all possible measures to minimize the distress.

4. The ethical researcher instructs research participants that they are free to withdraw their consent and from participation at any time.

5. The ethical researcher understands that information obtained about research participants during the course of an investigation is confidential. When the possibility exists that others may obtain access to such information, the participant must be made aware of the possibility and the plans for protecting confidentiality as a part of the procedure for obtaining informed consent.

6. The ethical researcher gives sponsoring agencies, host institutions, and publication channels the same respect and opportunity for informed consent that they accord to individual research participants.

7. The ethical researcher is aware of his or her obligation to future research workers and ensures that host institutions are given feedback information and proper acknowledgement.

Principle 6   Consulting

A) Mental health counselors acting as consultants must have a high degree of self-awareness of their own values, knowledge, skills and needs in entering a helping relationship that involves human and/or organizational change. The focus of the consulting relationship should be on the issues to be resolved and not on the personal characteristics of those presenting the consulting issues.

B) Mental health counselors should develop an understanding of the problem presented by the client and should secure an agreement with the consultation client, specifying the terms and nature of the consulting relationship.

C) Mental health counselors must be reasonably certain that they and their clients have the competencies and resources necessary to follow the consultation plan.

D) Mental health counselors should encourage adaptability and growth toward self-direction. Mental health counselors should avoid becoming a decision-maker or substitute for the client.

E) When announcing consultant availability for services, mental health counselors conscientiously adhere to professional standards.

F) Mental health counselors keep all proprietary information confidential.

G) Mental health counselors avoid conflicts of interest in selecting consultation clients

Professional Issues

Principle 7   Competence

The maintenance of high standards of professional competence is a responsibility shared by all mental health counselors in the best interests of the public and the profession. Mental health counselors recognize the boundaries of their particular competencies and the limitations of their expertise. Mental health counselors only provide those services and use only those techniques for which they are qualified by education, techniques or experience. Mental health counselors maintain knowledge of relevant scientific and professional information related to the services they render, and they recognize the need for on-going education.

A) Mental health counselors accurately represent their competence, education, training and experience.

B) As teaching professionals, mental health counselors perform their duties based on careful preparation in order that their instruction is accurate, up to date and educational.

C) Mental health counselors recognize the need for continued education and training in the area of cultural diversity and competency. Mental health counselors are open to new procedures and sensitive to the diversity of varying populations and changes in expectations and values over time.

D) Mental health counselors and practitioners recognize that their effectiveness depends in part upon their ability to maintain sound and healthy interpersonal relationships. They are aware that any unhealthy activity would compromise sound professional judgement and competency. In the event that personal problems arise and are affecting professional services, they will seek competent professional assistance to determine whether they should limit, suspend or terminate services to their clients.

E) Mental health counselors have a responsibility both to the individual who is served and to the institution within which the service is performed to maintain high standards of professional conduct. Mental health counselors strive to maintain the highest level of professional services offered to the agency, organization or institution in providing the highest caliber of professional services. The acceptance of employment in an institution implies that the mental health counselor is in substantial agreement with the general policies and principles of the institution. If, despite concerted efforts, the member cannot reach an agreement with the employer as to acceptable standards of conduct that allows for changes in institutional policy conducive to the positive growth and development of counselors, then terminating the affiliation should be seriously considered.

G) Ethical behavior among professional associates, mental health counselors and non-mental health counselors is expected at all times. When information is possessed that raises serious doubts as to the ethical behavior of professional colleagues, whether association members or not, the mental health counselor is obligated to take action to attempt to rectify such a condition. Such action shall utilize the institution's channels first and then utilize procedures established by the state licensure board.

H) Mental health counselors are aware of the intimacy of the counseling relationship, maintain a healthy respect for the integrity of the client, and avoid engaging in activities that seek to meet the mental health counselor's personal needs at the expense of the client. Through awareness of the negative impact of both racial and sexual stereotyping and discrimination, the member strives to ensure the individual rights and personal dignity of the client in the counseling relationship.

Principle 8 Professional Relationships

Mental health counselors act with due regard for the needs and feelings of their colleagues in counseling and other professions. Mental health counselors respect the prerogatives and obligations of the institutions or organizations with which they associate.

A) Mental health counselors understand how related professions complement their work and make full use of other professional, technical, and administrative resources that best serve the interests of consumers. The absence of formal relationships with other professional workers does not relieve mental health counselors from the responsibility of securing for their clients the best possible professional services; indeed, this circumstance presents a challenge to the professional competence of mental health counselors, requiring special sensitivity to problems outside their areas of training, and foresight, diligence, and tact in obtaining the professional assistance needed by clients.

B) Mental health counselors know and take into account the traditions and practices of other professional groups with which they work and cooperate fully with members of such groups when research, services and other functions are shared, or in working for the benefit of public welfare.

C) Mental health counselors treat professional colleagues with the same dignity and respect afforded to clients. Professional discourse should be free of personal attacks.

D) Mental health counselors strive to provide positive conditions for those they employ and to spell out clearly the conditions of such employment. They encourage their employees to engage in activities that facilitate their further professional development.

E) Mental health counselors respect the viability, reputation, and proprietary rights of organizations that they serve. Mental health counselors show due regard for the interest of their present or perspective employers. In those instances where they are critical of policies, they attempt to effect change by constructive action within the organization.

F) In pursuit of research, mental health counselors are to give sponsoring agencies, host institutions, and publication channels the same respect and opportunity for giving informed consent that they accord to individual research participants. They are aware of their obligation to future research workers and insure that host institutions are given feedback information and proper acknowledgement.

G) Credit is assigned to those who have contributed to a publication, in proportion to their contribution.

H) Mental health counselors do not accept or offer referral fees from other professionals.

I) When mental health counselors violate ethical standards, mental health counselors who know firsthand of such activities should, if possible, attempt to rectify the situation. Failing an informal solution, mental health counselors should bring such unethical activities to the attention of the appropriate state licensure board committee on ethics and professional conduct. Only after all professional alternatives have been utilized will mental health counselors begin legal action for resolution.

Principle 9 Supervisee, Student and Employee Relationships

Mental health counselors have an ethical concern for the integrity and welfare of supervisees, students, and employees. They maintain these relationships on a professional and confidential basis. They recognize the influential position they have with regard to both current and former supervisees, students and employees. They avoid exploiting their trust and dependency.

A) Mental health counselors do not engage in ongoing counseling relationships with current supervisees, students and employees.

B) All forms of sexual behavior with supervisees, students and employees are unethical. Further, mental health counselors do not engage in sexual or other harassment of supervisees, students, employees or colleagues.

C) Mental health counselor supervisors advise their supervisees, students and employees against offering or engaging in or holding themselves out as competent to engage in professional services beyond their training, level of experience and competence.

D) Mental health counselors make every effort to avoid dual relationships with supervisees, students and employees that could impair their judgment or increase the risk of personal or financial exploitation. When a dual relationship can not be avoided, mental health counselors take appropriate professional precautions to make sure that judgment is not impaired. Examples of such dual relationships include, but are not limited to, a supervisee who receives supervision as a benefit of employment, or a student in a small college where the only available counselor on campus is an instructor.

E) Mental health counselors do not disclose supervisee confidences except:

1. To prevent clear and eminent danger to a person or persons.

2. As mandated by law. a) As in mandated child or senior abuse reporting. b) Where the counselor is a defendant in a civil, criminal or disciplinary action. c) In educational or training settings where only other professionals who will share responsibility for the training of the supervisee are present. d) Where there is a waiver of confidentiality obtained in writing prior to such a release of information.

F) Supervisees must make their clients aware in their informed consent statement that they are under supervision and they must provide their clients with the name and credentials of their supervisor.

G) Mental health counselors require their supervisees, students and employees to adhere to the Code of Ethics. Students and supervisees have the same obligations to clients as those required of mental health counselors.

Principle 10 Moral and Legal Standards

Mental health counselors recognize that they have a moral, legal and ethical responsibility to the community and to the general public. Mental health counselors should be aware of the prevailing community standards and the impact of professional standards on the community.

A) To protect students, mental health counselors/teachers will be aware of diverse backgrounds of students and will see that material is treated objectively and fairly to reflect the multicultural community in which they live.

B) Providers of counseling services conform to the statutes relating to such services as established by their state and its regulating professional board(s).

C) As employees, mental health counselors refuse to participate in an employer's practices that are inconsistent with the moral and legal standards established by federal or state legislation regarding the treatment of employees. In particular and for example, mental health counselors will not condone practices that result in illegal or otherwise unjustified discrimination on the basis of race, sex, religion or national origin in hiring, promotion or training.

D) In providing counseling services to clients, mental health counselors avoid any action that will violate or diminish the legal and civil rights of clients or of others that may be effected by the action.

E) Sexual conduct, not limited to sexual intercourse, between mental health counselors and clients is specifically in violation of this Code of Ethics. This does not, however, prohibit the use of explicit instructional aids including films and videotapes. Such use is within excepted practices of trained and competent sex therapists.

Principle 11 Professional Responsibility

In their commitment to the understanding of human behavior, mental health counselors value objectivity and integrity, and in providing services they maintain the highest standards. They accept responsibility for the consequences of their work and make every effort to ensure that their services are used appropriately.

A) Mental health counselors accept ultimate responsibility for selecting appropriate areas for investigation and the methods relevant to minimize the possibility that their finding will be misleading. They provide thorough discussion of the limitations of their data and alternative hypotheses, especially where their work touches on social policy or might be misconstrued to the detriment of specific age, sex, ethnic, socioeconomic, or other social categories. In publishing reports of their work, they never discard observations that may modify the interpretation of results. Mental health counselors take credit only for the work they have actually done. In pursuing research, mental health counselors ascertain that their efforts will not lead to changes in individuals or organizations unless such changes are part of the agreement at the time of obtaining informed consent. Mental health counselors clarify in advance the expectations for sharing and utilizing research data. They avoid dual relationships that may limit objectivity, whether theoretical, political, or monetary, so that interference with data, subjects, and milieu is kept to a minimum.

B) As employees of an institution or agency, mental health counselors have the responsibility to remain alert to institutional pressures that may distort reports of counseling findings or use them in ways counter to the promotion of human welfare.

C) When serving as members of governmental or other organizational bodies, mental health counselors remain accountable as individuals to the Code of Ethics of the American Mental Health Counselors Association.

D) As teachers, mental health counselors recognize their primary obligation to help others acquire knowledge and skill. They maintain high standards of scholarship and objectivity by presenting counseling information fully and accurately, and by giving appropriate recognition to alternative viewpoints.

E) As practitioners, mental health counselors know that they bear a heavy social responsibility because their recommendations and professional actions may alter the lives of others. They therefore remained fully cognizant of their impact and alert to personal, social, organizational, financial or political situations or pressures that might lead to the misuse of their influence.

F) Mental health counselors provide reasonable and timely feedback to employees, trainees, supervisors, students, clients, and others whose work they may evaluate.

Principle 12 Private Practice

A) A mental health counselor should assist, where permitted by legislation or judicial decision, the profession in fulfilling its duty to make counseling services available in private settings.

B) In advertising services as a private practitioner, mental health counselors should advertise the services in such a manner so as to accurately inform the public as to services, expertise, profession, and techniques of counseling in a professional manner. Mental health counselors who assume an executive leadership role in the organization shall not permit their name to be used in professional notices during periods when not actively engaged in the private practice of counseling. Mental health counselors advertise the following: highest relevant degree, type and level of certification or license, and type and/or description of services or other relevant information. Such information should not contain false, inaccurate, misleading, partial, out of context, descriptive material or statements.

C) Mental health counselors may join in partnership/corporation with other mental health counselors and/or other professionals provided that each mental health counselor of the partnership or corporation makes clear his/her separate specialties, buying name in compliance with the regulations of the locality.

D) Mental health counselors have an obligation to withdraw from an employment relationship or a counseling relationship if it is believed that employment will result in violation of the Code of Ethics, if their mental capacity or physical condition renders it difficult to carry out an effective professional relationship, or if the mental health counselor is discharged by the client because the counseling relationship is no longer productive for the client.

E) Mental health counselors should adhere and support the regulations for private practice in the locality where the services are offered.

F) Mental health counselors refrain from attempts to utilize one's institutional affiliation to recruit clients for one's private practice. Mental health counselors are to refrain from offering their services in the private sector when they are employed by an institution in which this is prohibited by stated policy that reflects conditions of employment.

Principle 13 Public Statements

Mental health counselors in their professional roles may be expected or required to make public statements providing counseling information or professional opinions; or supply information about the availability of counseling products and services. In making such statements, mental health counselors take into full account the limits and uncertainties of present counseling knowledge and techniques. They represent, as accurately and objectively as possible, their professional qualifications, expertise, affiliations, and functions, as well as those of the institutions or organizations with which the statements may be associated. All public statements, announcements of services, and promotional activities should serve the purpose of providing sufficient information to aid the consumer public in making informed judgements and choices on matters that concern it. When announcing professional counseling services, mental health counselors may describe or explain those services offered but may not evaluate as to their quality or uniqueness and do not allow for testimonials by implication. All public statements should be otherwise consistent with this Code of Ethics.

Principle 14 Internet On-Line Counseling

Mental health counselors engaged in delivery of services that involves the telephone, teleconferencing and the Internet in which these areas are generally recognized, standards for preparatory training do not yet exist. Mental health counselors take responsible steps to ensure the competence of their work and protect patients, clients, students, research participants and others from harm.

A) Confidentiality
Mental health counselors ensure that clients are provided sufficient information to adequately address and explain the limitations of computer technology in the counseling process in general and the difficulties of ensuring complete client confidentiality of information transmitted through electronic communications over the Internet through on-line counseling. Professional counselors inform clients of the limitations of confidentiality and iden-

tify foreseeable situations in which confidentiality must be breached in light of the law in both the state in which the client is located and the state in which the professional counselor is licensed. Mental health counselors shall become aware of the means for reporting and protecting suicidal clients in their locale. Mental health counselors shall become aware of the means for reporting homicidal clients in the client's jurisdiction.

B) Mental Health Counselor Identification
Mental health counselors provide a readily visible notice advising clients of the identities of all professional counselor(s) who will have access to the information transmitted by the client. Mental health counselors provide background information on all professional communications, including education, licensing and certification, and practice information.

C) Client Identification
Professional counselors identify clients, verify identities of clients, and obtain alternative methods of contacting clients in emergency situations.

D) Client Waiver
Mental health counselors require clients to execute client waiver agreements stating that the client acknowledges the limitations inherent in ensuring client confidentiality of information transmitted through on-line counseling and acknowledge the limitations that are inherent in a counseling process that is not provided face-to-face. Limited training in the area of on-line counseling must be explained and the client's informed consent must be secured.

E) Electronic Transfer of Client Information
Mental health counselors electronically transfer client confidential information to authorized third-party recipients only when both the professional counselor and the authorized recipient have "secure" transfer and acceptance communication capabilities; the recipient is able to effectively protect the confidentiality of the client's confidential information to be transferred; and the informed written consent of the client, acknowledging the limits of confidentiality, has been obtained.

F) Establishing the On-Line Counseling Relationship
1. Appropriateness of On-line Counseling
Mental health counselors develop an appropriate intake procedure for potential clients to determine whether on-line counseling is appropriate for the needs of the client. Mental health counselors warn potential clients that on-line counseling services may not be appropriate in certain situations and, to the extent possible, inform the client of specific limitations, potential risks, and/or potential benefits relevant to the client's anticipated use of on-line counseling services. Mental health counselors ensure that clients are intellectually, emotionally, and physically capable of using on-line counseling services, and of understanding the potential risks and/or limitations of such services.

2. Counseling Plans
Mental health counselors develop individual on-line counseling plans that are consistent with both the client's individual circumstances and the limitations of on-line counseling. Mental health counselors who determine that on-line counseling is inappropriate for the client should avoid entering into or immediately terminate the on-line counseling relationship and encourage the client to continue the counseling relationship through a traditional alternative method of counseling.

3. Boundaries of Competence
Mental health counselors provide on-line counseling services only in practice areas within their expertise. Mental health counselors do not provide services to clients in states where doing so would violate local licensure laws or regulations.

G) Legal Considerations
Mental health counselors confirm that the provision of on-line services are not prohibited by or otherwise violate any applicable state or local statutes, rules, regulations or ordinances, codes of professional membership organizations and certifying boards, and/or codes of state licensing boards.

Principle 15   Resolution of Ethical Problems

Neither the American Mental Health Counselors Association, its Board of Directors, nor its National Committee on Ethics investigate or adjudicate ethical complaints. In the event a member has his or her license suspended or revoked by an appropriate state licensure board, the AMHCA Board of Directors may then act in accordance with AMHCA's National By-Laws to suspend or revoke his or her membership.

Any member so suspended may apply for reinstatement upon the reinstatement of his or her licensure.

CHAPTER 8

Code of Ethics of the National Association of Social Workers (1999)

The *Code of Ethics of the National Association of Social Workers* (NASW) is meant to articulate the basic values, ethical principles, and ethical standards of social work and to be relevant to social workers and social work students regardless of their professional setting, functions, or populations served (Rothman, 2004) . The code is rooted in a set of core values that are the foundation on which social work is built. These values are service, social justice, dignity and worth of the person, importance of human relationships, integrity, and competence.

The *Code of Ethics of NASW* includes a Preamble, a Purpose, Ethical Principles, and six (6) Ethical Standards. The Ethical Standards are both enforceable guidelines for professional conduct and aspirations. They all are prefaced by the words "Social Workers' Ethical Responsibilities" and include these obligations:

- to Clients
- to Colleagues
- in Practice Settings
- as Professionals
- to the Social Work Profession
- to the Broader Society

As with the *Code of Ethics of the AMHCA*, the *Code of Ethics of NASW* includes more subsections (N = 16) under its standards for work related to clients than it does under other standards. Unlike the AMHCA code, however, the NASW code does not include a section on resolving ethical problems. Instead, like most other ethical codes, the NASW code refers the reader to a separate publication on procedures for the adjudication of grievances. The *Code of Ethics of NASW* points out in its purpose section that reasonable differences may exist among social workers regarding ethics. Thus, it reminds social work practitioners that the resolution of ethical issues may be most complex at times and may involve considerable discussion.

Reference:

Rotheman, J. C. (2004). *From the front lines: Student cases in social work ethics (*2nd Ed.). Boston: Allyn & Bacon.

CODE OF ETHICS OF THE NATIONAL ASSOCIATION OF SOCIAL WORKERS

(Approved by the 1996 NASW Delegate Assembly and revised by the 1999 NASW Delegate Assembly)

PREAMBLE

The primary mission of the social work profession is to enhance human well-being and help meet the basic human needs of all people, with particular attention to the needs and empowerment of people who are vulnerable, oppressed, and living in poverty. A historic and defining feature of social work is the profession's focus on individual well-being in a social context and the well-being of society. Fundamental to social work is attention to the environmental forces that create, contribute to, and address problems in living.

Social workers promote social justice and social change with and on behalf of clients. "Clients" is used inclusively to refer to individuals, families, groups, organizations, and communities. Social workers are sensitive to cultural and ethnic diversity and strive to end discrimination, oppression, poverty, and other forms of social injustice. These activities may be in the form of direct practice, community organizing, supervision, consultation, administration, advocacy, social and political action, policy development and implementation, education, and research and evaluation. Social workers seek to enhance the capacity of people to address their own needs. Social workers also seek to promote the responsiveness of organizations, communities, and other social institutions to individuals' needs and social problems.

The mission of the social work profession is rooted in a set of core values. These core values, embraced by social workers throughout the profession's history, are the foundation of social work's unique purpose and perspective:

- service
- social justice
- dignity and worth of the person
- importance of human relationships
- integrity
- competence

This constellation of core values reflects what is unique to the social work profession. Core values, and the principles that flow from them, must be balanced within the context and complexity of the human experience.

Purpose of the NASW Code of Ethics

Professional ethics are at the core of social work. The profession has an obligation to articulate its basic values, ethical principles, and ethical standards. The NASW Code of Ethics sets forth these values, principles, and standards to guide social workers' conduct. The Code is relevant to all social workers and social work students, regardless of their professional functions, the settings in which they work, or the populations they serve.

The NASW Code of Ethics serves six purposes:

1. The Code identifies core values on which social work's mission is based.
2. The Code summarizes broad ethical principles that reflect the profession's core values and establishes a set of specific ethical standards that should be used to guide social work practice.
3. The Code is designed to help social workers identify relevant considerations when professional obligations conflict or ethical uncertainties arise.
4. The Code provides ethical standards to which the general public can hold the social work profession accountable.
5. The Code socializes practitioners new to the field to social work's mission, values, ethical principles, and ethical standards.
6. The Code articulates standards that the social work profession itself can use to assess whether social workers have engaged in unethical conduct. NASW has formal procedures to adjudicate ethics complaints filed against its members.* In subscribing to this Code, social workers are required to cooperate in its implementation, participate in NASW adjudication proceedings, and abide by any NASW disciplinary rulings or sanctions based on it.

*For information on NASW adjudication procedures, see NASW Procedures for the Adjudication of Grievances.

The Code offers a set of values, principles, and standards to guide decision making and conduct when ethical issues arise. It does not provide a set of rules that prescribe how social workers should act in all situations.

Specific applications of the Code must take into account the context in which it is being considered and the possibility of conflicts among the Code's values, principles, and standards. Ethical responsibilities flow from all human relationships, from the personal and familial to the social and professional.

Further, the NASW Code of Ethics does not specify which values, principles, and standards are most important and ought to outweigh others in instances when they conflict. Reasonable differences of opinion can and do exist among social workers with respect to the ways in which values, ethical principles, and ethical standards should be rank ordered when they conflict. Ethical decision making in a given situation must apply the informed judgment of the individual social worker and should also consider how the issues would be judged in a peer review process where the ethical standards of the profession would be applied.

Ethical decision making is a process. There are many instances in social work where simple answers are not available to resolve complex ethical issues. Social workers should take into consideration all the values, principles, and standards in this *Code* that are relevant to any situation in which ethical judgment is warranted. Social workers' decisions and actions should be consistent with the spirit as well as the letter of this *Code*.

In addition to this *Code*, there are many other sources of information about ethical thinking that may be useful. Social workers should consider ethical theory and principles generally, social work theory and research, laws, regulations, agency policies, and other relevant codes of ethics, recognizing that among codes of ethics social workers should consider the *NASW Code of Ethics* as their primary source. Social workers also should be aware of the impact on ethical decision making of their clients' and their own personal values and cultural and religious beliefs and practices. They should be aware of any conflicts between personal and professional values and deal with them responsibly. For additional guidance social workers should consult the relevant literature on professional ethics and ethical decision making and seek appropriate consultation when faced with ethical dilemmas. This may involve consultation with an agency-based or social work organization's ethics committee, a regulatory body, knowledgeable colleagues, supervisors, or legal counsel.

Instances may arise when social workers' ethical obligations conflict with agency policies or relevant laws or regulations. When such conflicts occur, social workers must make a responsible effort to resolve the conflict in a manner that is consistent with the values, principles, and standards expressed in this *Code*. If a reasonable resolution of the conflict does not appear possible, social workers should seek proper consultation before making a decision.

The *NASW Code of Ethics* is to be used by NASW and by individuals, agencies, organizations, and bodies (such as licensing and regulatory boards, professional liability insurance providers, courts of law, agency boards of directors, government agencies, and other professional groups) that choose to adopt it or use it as a frame of reference. Violation of standards in this *Code* does not automatically imply legal liability or violation of the law. Such determination can only be made in the context of legal and judicial proceedings. Alleged violations of the *Code* would be subject to a peer review process. Such processes are generally separate from legal or administrative procedures and insulated from legal review or proceedings to allow the profession to counsel and discipline its own members.

A code of ethics cannot guarantee ethical behavior. Moreover, a code of ethics cannot resolve all ethical issues or disputes or capture the richness and complexity involved in striving to make responsible choices within a moral community. Rather, a code of ethics sets forth values, ethical principles, and ethical standards to which professionals aspire and by which their actions can be judged. Social workers' ethical behavior should result from their personal commitment to engage in ethical practice. The *NASW Code of Ethics* reflects the commitment of all social workers to uphold the profession's values and to act ethically. Principles and standards must be applied by individuals of good character who discern moral questions and, in good faith, seek to make reliable ethical judgments.

Ethical Principles

The following broad ethical principles are based on social work's core values of service, social justice, dignity and worth of the person, importance of human relationships, integrity, and competence. These principles set forth ideals to which all social workers should aspire.

Value: *Service*

Ethical Principle: *Social workers' primary goal is to help people in need and to address social problems.*

Social workers elevate service to others above self-interest. Social workers draw on their knowledge, values, and skills to help people in need and to address social problems. Social workers are encouraged to volunteer some portion of their professional skills with no expectation of significant financial return (pro bono service).

Value: *Social Justice*

Ethical Principle: *Social workers challenge social injustice.*

Social workers pursue social change, particularly with and on behalf of vulnerable and oppressed individuals and groups of people. Social workers' social change efforts are focused primarily on issues of poverty, unemployment, discrimination, and other forms of social injustice. These activities seek to promote sensitivity to and knowledge about oppression and cultural and ethnic diversity. Social workers strive to ensure access to needed information, services, and resources; equality of opportunity; and meaningful participation in decision making for all people.

Value: *Dignity and Worth of the Person*

Ethical Principle: *Social workers respect the inherent dignity and worth of the person.*

Social workers treat each person in a caring and respectful fashion, mindful of individual differences and cultural and ethnic diversity. Social workers promote clients' socially responsible self-determination. Social workers seek to enhance clients' capacity and opportunity to change and to address their own needs. Social workers are cognizant of their dual responsibility to clients and to the broader society. They seek to resolve conflicts between clients' interests and the broader society's interests in a socially responsible manner consistent with the values, ethical principles, and ethical standards of the profession.

Value: *Importance of Human Relationships*

Ethical Principle: *Social workers recognize the central importance of human relationships.*

Social workers understand that relationships between and among people are an important vehicle for change. Social workers engage people as partners in the helping process. Social workers seek to strengthen relationships among people in a purposeful effort to promote, restore, maintain, and enhance the well-being of individuals, families, social groups, organizations, and communities.

Value: *Integrity*

Ethical Principle: *Social workers behave in a trustworthy manner.*

Social workers are continually aware of the profession's mission, values, ethical principles, and ethical standards and practice in a manner consistent with them. Social workers act honestly and responsibly and promote ethical practices on the part of the organizations with which they are affiliated.

Value: *Competence*

Ethical Principle: *Social workers practice within their areas of competence and develop and enhance their professional expertise.*

Social workers continually strive to increase their professional knowledge and skills and to apply them in practice. Social workers should aspire to contribute to the knowledge base of the profession.

Ethical Standards

The following ethical standards are relevant to the professional activities of all social workers. These standards concern (1) social workers' ethical responsibilities to clients, (2) social workers' ethical responsibilities to colleagues, (3) social workers' ethical responsibilities in practice settings, (4) social workers' ethical responsibilities as professionals, (5) social workers' ethical responsibilities to the social work profession, and (6) social workers' ethical responsibilities to the broader society.

Some of the standards that follow are enforceable guidelines for professional conduct, and some are aspirational. The extent to which each standard is enforceable is a matter of professional judgment to be exercised by those responsible for reviewing alleged violations of ethical standards.

1. Social Workers' Ethical Responsibilities to Clients

1.01 Commitment to Clients
Social workers' primary responsibility is to promote the well-being of clients. In general, clients' interests are primary. However, social workers' responsibility to the larger society or specific legal obligations may on limited occasions supersede the loyalty owed clients, and clients should be so advised. (Examples include when a social worker is required by law to report that a client has abused a child or has threatened to harm self or others.)

1.02 Self-Determination
Social workers respect and promote the right of clients to self-determination and assist clients in their efforts to identify and clarify their goals. Social workers may limit clients' right to self-determination when, in the social workers' professional judgment, clients' actions or potential actions pose a serious, foreseeable, and imminent risk to themselves or others.

1.03 Informed Consent
(a) Social workers should provide services to clients only in the context of a professional relationship based, when appropriate, on valid informed consent. Social workers should use clear and understandable language to inform clients of the purpose of the services, risks related to the services, limits to services because of the requirements of a third-party payer, relevant costs, reasonable alternatives, clients' right to refuse or withdraw consent, and the time frame covered by the consent. Social workers should provide clients with an opportunity to ask questions.

(b) In instances when clients are not literate or have difficulty understanding the primary language used in the practice setting, social workers should take steps to ensure clients' comprehension. This may include providing clients with a detailed verbal explanation or arranging for a qualified interpreter or translator whenever possible.

(c) In instances when clients lack the capacity to provide informed consent, social workers should protect clients' interests by seeking permission from an appropriate third party, informing clients consistent with the clients' level of understanding. In such instances social workers should seek to ensure that the third party acts in a manner consistent with clients' wishes and interests. Social workers should take reasonable steps to enhance such clients' ability to give informed consent.

(d) In instances when clients are receiving services involuntarily, social workers should provide information about the nature and extent of services and about the extent of clients' right to refuse service.

(e) Social workers who provide services via electronic media (such as computer, telephone, radio, and television) should inform recipients of the limitations and risks associated with such services.

(f) Social workers should obtain clients' informed consent before audiotaping or videotaping clients or permitting observation of services to clients by a third party.

1.04 Competence

(a) Social workers should provide services and represent themselves as competent only within the boundaries of their education, training, license, certification, consultation received, supervised experience, or other relevant professional experience.

(b) Social workers should provide services in substantive areas or use intervention techniques or approaches that are new to them only after engaging in appropriate study, training, consultation, and supervision from people who are competent in those interventions or techniques.

(c) When generally recognized standards do not exist with respect to an emerging area of practice, social workers should exercise careful judgment and take responsible steps (including appropriate education, research, training, consultation, and supervision) to ensure the competence of their work and to protect clients from harm.

1.05 Cultural Competence and Social Diversity

(a) Social workers should understand culture and its function in human behavior and society, recognizing the strengths that exist in all cultures.

(b) Social workers should have a knowledge base of their clients' cultures and be able to demonstrate competence in the provision of services that are sensitive to clients' cultures and to differences among people and cultural groups.

(c) Social workers should obtain education about and seek to understand the nature of social diversity and

oppression with respect to race, ethnicity, national origin, color, sex, sexual orientation, age, marital status, political belief, religion, and mental or physical disability.

1.06 Conflicts of Interest

(a) Social workers should be alert to and avoid conflicts of interest that interfere with the exercise of professional discretion and impartial judgment. Social workers should inform clients when a real or potential conflict of interest arises and take reasonable steps to resolve the issue in a manner that makes the clients' interests primary and protects clients' interests to the greatest extent possible. In some cases, protecting clients' interests may require ter-

mination of the professional relationship with proper referral of the client.

(b) Social workers should not take unfair advantage of any professional relationship or exploit others to further their personal, religious, political, or business interests.

(c) Social workers should not engage in dual or multiple relationships with clients or former clients in which there is a risk of exploitation or potential harm to the client. In instances when dual or multiple relationships are unavoidable, social workers should take steps to protect clients and are responsible for setting clear, appropriate, and culturally sensitive boundaries. (Dual or multiple relationships occur when social workers relate to clients in more than one relationship, whether professional, social, or business. Dual or multiple relationships can occur simultaneously or consecutively.)

(d) When social workers provide services to two or more people who have a relationship with each other (for example, couples, family members), social workers should clarify with all parties which individuals will be considered clients and the nature of social workers' professional obligations to the various individuals who are receiving services. Social workers who anticipate a conflict of interest among the individuals receiving services or who anticipate having to perform in potentially conflicting roles (for example, when a social worker is asked to testify in a child custody dispute or divorce proceedings involving clients) should clarify their role with the parties involved and take appropriate action to minimize any conflict of interest.

1.07 Privacy and Confidentiality

(a) Social workers should respect clients' right to privacy. Social workers should not solicit private information from clients unless it is essential to providing services or conducting social work evaluation or research. Once private information is shared, standards of confidentiality apply.

(b) Social workers may disclose confidential information when appropriate with valid consent from a client or a person legally authorized to consent on behalf of a client.

(c) Social workers should protect the confidentiality of all information obtained in the course of professional service, except for compelling professional reasons. The general expectation that social workers will keep information confidential does not apply when disclosure is necessary to prevent serious, foreseeable, and imminent harm to a client or other identifiable person. In all instances, social workers should disclose the least amount of confidential information necessary to achieve the desired purpose; only information that is directly relevant to the purpose for which the disclosure is made should be revealed.

(d) Social workers should inform clients, to the extent possible, about the disclosure of confidential information and the potential consequences, when feasible before the disclosure is made. This applies whether social workers disclose confidential information on the basis of a legal requirement or client consent.

(e) Social workers should discuss with clients and other interested parties the nature of confidentiality and limitations of clients' right to confidentiality. Social workers should review with clients circumstances where confidential information may be requested and where disclosure of confidential information may be legally required. This discussion should occur as soon as possible in the social worker-client relationship and as needed throughout the course of the relationship.

(f) When social workers provide counseling services to families, couples, or groups, social workers should seek agreement among the parties involved concerning each individual's right to confidentiality and obligation to preserve the confidentiality of information shared by others. Social workers should inform participants in family, couples, or group counseling that social workers cannot guarantee that all participants will honor such agreements.

(g) Social workers should inform clients involved in family, couples, marital, or group counseling of the social worker's, employer's, and agency's policy concerning the social worker's disclosure of confidential information among the parties involved in the counseling.

(h) Social workers should not disclose confidential information to third-party payers unless clients have authorized such disclosure.

(i) Social workers should not discuss confidential information in any setting unless privacy can be ensured. Social workers should not discuss confidential information in public or semipublic areas such as hallways, waiting rooms, elevators, and restaurants.

(j) Social workers should protect the confidentiality of clients during legal proceedings to the extent permitted by law. When a court of law or other legally authorized body orders social workers to disclose confidential or privileged information without a client's consent and such disclosure could cause harm to the client, social workers should request that the court withdraw the order or limit the order as narrowly as possible or maintain the records under seal, unavailable for public inspection.

(k) Social workers should protect the confidentiality of clients when responding to requests from members of the media.

(l) Social workers should protect the confidentiality of clients' written and electronic records and other sensitive information. Social workers should take reasonable steps to ensure that clients' records are stored in a secure location and that clients' records are not available to others who are not authorized to have access.

(m) Social workers should take precautions to ensure and maintain the confidentiality of information transmitted to other parties through the use of computers, electronic mail, facsimile machines, telephones and telephone answering machines, and other electronic or computer technology. Disclosure of identifying information should be avoided whenever possible.

(n) Social workers should transfer or dispose of clients' records in a manner that protects clients' confidentiality and is consistent with state statutes governing records and social work licensure.

(o) Social workers should take reasonable precautions to protect client confidentiality in the event of the social worker's termination of practice, incapacitation, or death.

(p) Social workers should not disclose identifying information when discussing clients for teaching or training purposes unless the client has consented to disclosure of confidential information.

(q) Social workers should not disclose identifying information when discussing clients with consultants unless the client has consented to disclosure of confidential information or there is a compelling need for such disclosure.

(r) Social workers should protect the confidentiality of deceased clients consistent with the preceding standards.

1.08 Access to Records

(a) Social workers should provide clients with reasonable access to records concerning the clients. Social workers who are concerned that clients' access to their records could cause serious misunderstanding or harm to the client should provide assistance in interpreting the records and consultation with the client regarding the records. Social workers should limit clients' access to their records, or portions of their records, only in exceptional circumstances when there is compelling evidence that such access would cause serious harm to the client. Both clients' requests and the rationale for withholding some or all of the record should be documented in clients' files.

(b) When providing clients with access to their records, social workers should take steps to protect the confidentiality of other individuals identified or discussed in such records.

1.09 Sexual Relationships

(a) Social workers should under no circumstances engage in sexual activities or sexual contact with current clients, whether such contact is consensual or forced.

(b) Social workers should not engage in sexual activities or sexual contact with clients' relatives or other individuals with whom clients maintain a close personal relationship when there is a risk of exploitation or potential harm to the client. Sexual activity or sexual contact with clients' relatives or other individuals with whom clients maintain a personal relationship has the potential to be harmful to the client and may make it difficult for the social worker and client to maintain appropriate professional boundaries. Social workers--not their clients, their clients' relatives, or other individuals with whom the client maintains a personal relationship--assume the full burden for setting clear, appropriate, and culturally sensitive boundaries.

(c) Social workers should not engage in sexual activities or sexual contact with former clients because of the potential for harm to the client. If social workers engage in conduct contrary to this prohibition or claim that an exception to this prohibition is warranted because of extraordinary circumstances, it is social workers--not their clients--who assume the full burden of demonstrating that the former client has not been exploited, coerced, or manipulated, intentionally or unintentionally.

(d) Social workers should not provide clinical services to individuals with whom they have had a prior sexual relationship. Providing clinical services to a former sexual partner has the potential to be harmful to the individual and is likely to make it difficult for the social worker and individual to maintain appropriate professional boundaries.

1.10 Physical Contact

Social workers should not engage in physical contact with clients when there is a possibility of psychological harm to the client as a result of the contact (such as cradling or caressing clients). Social workers who engage in appropriate physical contact with clients are responsible for setting clear, appropriate, and culturally sensitive boundaries that govern such physical contact.

1.11 Sexual Harassment

Social workers should not sexually harass clients. Sexual harassment includes sexual advances, sexual solicitation, requests for sexual favors, and other verbal or physical conduct of a sexual nature.

1.12 Derogatory Language

Social workers should not use derogatory language in their written or verbal communications to or about clients. Social workers should use accurate and respectful language in all communications to and about clients.

1.13 Payment for Services

(a) When setting fees, social workers should ensure that the fees are fair, reasonable, and commensurate with the services performed. Consideration should be given to clients' ability to pay.

(b) Social workers should avoid accepting goods or services from clients as payment for professional services. Bartering arrangements, particularly involving services, create the potential for conflicts of interest, exploitation, and inappropriate boundaries in social workers' relationships with clients. Social workers should explore and may participate in bartering only in very limited circumstances when it can be demonstrated that such arrangements are an accepted practice among professionals in the local community, considered to be essential for the provision of services, negotiated without coercion, and entered into at the client's initiative and with the client's informed consent. Social workers who accept goods or services from clients as payment for professional services assume the full burden of demonstrating that this arrangement will not be detrimental to the client or the professional relationship.

(c) Social workers should not solicit a private fee or other remuneration for providing services to clients who are entitled to such available services through the social workers' employer or agency.

1.14 Clients Who Lack Decision-Making Capacity

When social workers act on behalf of clients who lack the capacity to make informed decisions, social workers should take reasonable steps to safeguard the interests and rights of those clients.

1.15 Interruption of Services

Social workers should make reasonable efforts to ensure continuity of services in the event that services are interrupted by factors such as unavailability, relocation, illness, disability, or death.

1.16 Termination of Services

(a) Social workers should terminate services to clients and professional relationships with them when such services and relationships are no longer required or no longer serve the clients' needs or interests.

(b) Social workers should take reasonable steps to avoid abandoning clients who are still in need of services. Social workers should withdraw services precipitously only under unusual circumstances, giving careful consideration to all factors in the situation and taking care to minimize possible adverse effects. Social workers should assist in making appropriate arrangements for continuation of services when necessary.

(c) Social workers in fee-for-service settings may terminate services to clients who are not paying an overdue balance if the financial contractual arrangements have been made clear to the client, if the client does not pose an imminent danger to self or others, and if the clinical and other consequences of the current nonpayment have been addressed and discussed with the client.

(d) Social workers should not terminate services to pursue a social, financial, or sexual relationship with a client.

(e) Social workers who anticipate the termination or interruption of services to clients should notify clients promptly and seek the transfer, referral, or continuation of services in relation to the clients' needs and preferences.

(f) Social workers who are leaving an employment setting should inform clients of appropriate options for the continuation of services and of the benefits and risks of the options.

2. Social Workers' Ethical Responsibilities to Colleagues

2.01 Respect
(a) Social workers should treat colleagues with respect and should represent accurately and fairly the qualifications, views, and obligations of colleagues.

(b) Social workers should avoid unwarranted negative criticism of colleagues in communications with clients or with other professionals. Unwarranted negative criticism may include demeaning comments that refer to colleagues' level of competence or to individuals' attributes such as race, ethnicity, national origin, color, sex, sexual orientation, age, marital status, political belief, religion, and mental or physical disability.

(c) Social workers should cooperate with social work colleagues and with colleagues of other professions when such cooperation serves the well-being of clients.

2.02 Confidentiality
Social workers should respect confidential information shared by colleagues in the course of their professional relationships and transactions. Social workers should ensure that such colleagues understand social workers' obligation to respect confidentiality and any exceptions related to it.

2.03 Interdisciplinary Collaboration
(a) Social workers who are members of an interdisciplinary team should participate in and contribute to decisions that affect the well-being of clients by drawing on the perspectives, values, and experiences of the social work profession. Professional and ethical obligations of the interdisciplinary team as a whole and of its individual members should be clearly established.

(b) Social workers for whom a team decision raises ethical concerns should attempt to resolve the disagreement through appropriate channels. If the disagreement cannot be resolved, social workers should pursue other avenues to address their concerns consistent with client well-being.

2.04 Disputes Involving Colleagues
(a) Social workers should not take advantage of a dispute between a colleague and an employer to obtain a position or otherwise advance the social workers' own interests.

(b) Social workers should not exploit clients in disputes with colleagues or engage clients in any inappropriate discussion of conflicts between social workers and their colleagues.

2.05 Consultation
(a) Social workers should seek the advice and counsel of colleagues whenever such consultation is in the best interests of clients.

(b) Social workers should keep themselves informed about colleagues' areas of expertise and competencies. Social workers should seek consultation only from colleagues who have demonstrated knowledge, expertise, and competence related to the subject of the consultation.

(c) When consulting with colleagues about clients, social workers should disclose the least amount of information necessary to achieve the purposes of the consultation.

2.06 Referral for Services
(a) Social workers should refer clients to other professionals when the other professionals' specialized knowledge or expertise is needed to serve clients fully or when social workers believe that they are not being effective or making reasonable progress with clients and that additional service is required.

(b) Social workers who refer clients to other professionals should take appropriate steps to facilitate an orderly transfer of responsibility. Social workers who refer clients to other professionals should disclose, with clients' consent, all pertinent information to the new service providers.

(c) Social workers are prohibited from giving or receiving payment for a referral when no professional service is provided by the referring social worker.

2.07 Sexual Relationships
(a) Social workers who function as supervisors or educators should not engage in sexual activities or contact with supervisees, students, trainees, or other colleagues over whom they exercise professional authority.

(b) Social workers should avoid engaging in sexual relationships with colleagues when there is potential for a conflict of interest. Social workers who become involved in, or anticipate becoming involved in, a sexual relationship with a colleague have a duty to transfer professional responsibilities, when necessary, to avoid a conflict of interest.

2.08 Sexual Harassment
Social workers should not sexually harass supervisees, students, trainees, or colleagues. Sexual harassment includes sexual advances, sexual solicitation, requests for sexual favors, and other verbal or physical conduct of a sexual nature.

2.09 Impairment of Colleagues
(a) Social workers who have direct knowledge of a social work colleague's impairment that is due to personal problems, psychosocial distress, substance abuse, or mental health difficulties and that interferes with practice effec-

tiveness should consult with that colleague when feasible and assist the colleague in taking remedial action.

(b) Social workers who believe that a social work colleague's impairment interferes with practice effectiveness and that the colleague has not taken adequate steps to address the impairment should take action through appropriate channels established by employers, agencies, NASW, licensing and regulatory bodies, and other professional organizations.

2.10 Incompetence of Colleagues
(a) Social workers who have direct knowledge of a social work colleague's incompetence should consult with that colleague when feasible and assist the colleague in taking remedial action.

(b) Social workers who believe that a social work colleague is incompetent and has not taken adequate steps to address the incompetence should take action through appropriate channels established by employers, agencies, NASW, licensing and regulatory bodies, and other professional organizations.

2.11 Unethical Conduct of Colleagues
(a) Social workers should take adequate measures to discourage, prevent, expose, and correct the unethical conduct of colleagues.

(b) Social workers should be knowledgeable about established policies and procedures for handling concerns about colleagues' unethical behavior. Social workers should be familiar with national, state, and local procedures for handling ethics complaints. These include policies and procedures created by NASW, licensing and regulatory bodies, employers, agencies, and other professional organizations.

(c) Social workers who believe that a colleague has acted unethically should seek resolution by discussing their concerns with the colleague when feasible and when such discussion is likely to be productive.

d) When necessary, social workers who believe that a colleague has acted unethically should take action through appropriate formal channels (such as contacting a state licensing board or regulatory body, an NASW committee on inquiry, or other professional ethics committees).

(e) Social workers should defend and assist colleagues who are unjustly charged with unethical conduct.

3. Social Workers' Ethical Responsibilities in Practice Settings

3.01 Supervision and Consultation
(a) Social workers who provide supervision or consultation should have the necessary knowledge and skill to supervise or consult appropriately and should do so only within their areas of knowledge and competence.

(b) Social workers who provide supervision or consultation are responsible for setting clear, appropriate, and culturally sensitive boundaries.

(c) Social workers should not engage in any dual or multiple relationships with supervisees in which there is a risk of exploitation of or potential harm to the supervisee.

(d) Social workers who provide supervision should evaluate supervisees' performance in a manner that is fair and respectful.

3.02 Education and Training
(a) Social workers who function as educators, field instructors for students, or trainers should provide instruction only within their areas of knowledge and competence and should provide instruction based on the most current information and knowledge available in the profession.

(b) Social workers who function as educators or field instructors for students should evaluate students' performance in a manner that is fair and respectful.

(c) Social workers who function as educators or field instructors for students should take reasonable steps to ensure that clients are routinely informed when services are being provided by students.

(d) Social workers who function as educators or field instructors for students should not engage in any dual or multiple relationships with students in which there is a risk of exploitation or potential harm to the student. Social work educators and field instructors are responsible for setting clear, appropriate, and culturally sensitive boundaries.

3.03 Performance Evaluation
Social workers who have responsibility for evaluating the performance of others should fulfill such responsibility in a fair and considerate manner and on the basis of clearly stated criteria.

3.04 Client Records
(a) Social workers should take reasonable steps to ensure that documentation in records is accurate and reflects the services provided.

(b) Social workers should include sufficient and timely documentation in records to facilitate the delivery of services and to ensure continuity of services provided to clients in the future.

(c) Social workers' documentation should protect clients' privacy to the extent that is possible and appropriate and should include only information that is directly relevant to the delivery of services.

(d) Social workers should store records following the termination of services to ensure reasonable future access. Records should be maintained for the number of years required by state statutes or relevant contracts.

3.05 Billing
Social workers should establish and maintain billing practices that accurately reflect the nature and extent of services provided and that identify who provided the service in the practice setting.

3.06 Client Transfer
(a) When an individual who is receiving services from another agency or colleague contacts a social worker for services, the social worker should carefully consider the client's needs before agreeing to provide services. To minimize possible confusion and conflict, social workers should discuss with potential clients the nature of the clients' current relationship with other service providers and the implications, including possible benefits or risks, of entering into a relationship with a new service provider.

(b) If a new client has been served by another agency or colleague, social workers should discuss with the client whether consultation with the previous service provider is in the client's best interest.

3.07 Administration
(a) Social work administrators should advocate within and outside their agencies for adequate resources to meet clients' needs.

(b) Social workers should advocate for resource allocation procedures that are open and fair. When not all clients' needs can be met, an allocation procedure should be developed that is nondiscriminatory and based on appropriate and consistently applied principles.

(c) Social workers who are administrators should take reasonable steps to ensure that adequate agency or organizational resources are available to provide appropriate staff supervision.

(d) Social work administrators should take reasonable steps to ensure that the working environment for which they are responsible is consistent with and encourages compliance with the NASW Code of Ethics. Social work administrators should take reasonable steps to eliminate any conditions in their organizations that violate, interfere with, or discourage compliance with the Code.

3.08 Continuing Education and Staff Development
Social work administrators and supervisors should take reasonable steps to provide or arrange for continuing education and staff development for all staff for whom they are responsible. Continuing education and staff development should address current knowledge and emerging developments related to social work practice and ethics.

3.09 Commitments to Employers
(a) Social workers generally should adhere to commitments made to employers and employing organizations.

(b) Social workers should work to improve employing agencies' policies and procedures and the efficiency and effectiveness of their services.

(c) Social workers should take reasonable steps to ensure that employers are aware of social workers' ethical obligations as set forth in the NASW Code of Ethics and of the implications of those obligations for social work practice.

(d) Social workers should not allow an employing organization's policies, procedures, regulations, or administrative orders to interfere with their ethical practice of social work. Social workers should take reasonable steps to ensure that their employing organizations' practices are consistent with the NASW Code of Ethics.

(e) Social workers should act to prevent and eliminate discrimination in the employing organization's work assignments and in its employment policies and practices.

(f) Social workers should accept employment or arrange student field placements only in organizations that exercise fair personnel practices.

(g) Social workers should be diligent stewards of the resources of their employing organizations, wisely conserving funds where appropriate and never misappropriating funds or using them for unintended purposes.

3.10 Labor-Management Disputes
(a) Social workers may engage in organized action, including the formation of and participation in labor unions, to improve services to clients and working conditions.

(b) The actions of social workers who are involved in labor-management disputes, job actions, or labor strikes should be guided by the profession's values, ethical principles, and ethical standards. Reasonable differences of opinion exist among social workers concerning their primary obligation as professionals during an actual or threatened labor strike or job action. Social workers should carefully examine relevant issues and their possible impact on clients before deciding on a course of action.

4. Social Workers' Ethical Responsibilities as Professionals

4.01 Competence
(a) Social workers should accept responsibility or employment only on the basis of existing competence or the intention to acquire the necessary competence.

(b) Social workers should strive to become and remain proficient in professional practice and the performance of professional functions. Social workers should critically examine and keep current with emerging knowledge relevant to social work. Social workers should routinely review the professional literature and participate in continuing education relevant to social work practice and social work ethics.

(c) Social workers should base practice on recognized knowledge, including empirically based knowledge, relevant to social work and social work ethics.

4.02 Discrimination

Social workers should not practice, condone, facilitate, or collaborate with any form of discrimination on the basis of race, ethnicity, national origin, color, sex, sexual orientation, age, marital status, political belief, religion, or mental or physical disability.

4.03 Private Conduct

Social workers should not permit their private conduct to interfere with their ability to fulfill their professional responsibilities.

4.04 Dishonesty, Fraud, and Deception

Social workers should not participate in, condone, or be associated with dishonesty, fraud, or deception.

4.05 Impairment

(a) Social workers should not allow their own personal problems, psychosocial distress, legal problems, substance abuse, or mental health difficulties to interfere with their professional judgment and performance or to jeopardize the best interests of people for whom they have a professional responsibility.

(b) Social workers whose personal problems, psychosocial distress, legal problems, substance abuse, or mental health difficulties interfere with their professional judgment and performance should immediately seek consultation and take appropriate remedial action by seeking professional help, making adjustments in workload, terminating practice, or taking any other steps necessary to protect clients and others.

4.06 Misrepresentation

(a) Social workers should make clear distinctions between statements made and actions engaged in as a private individual and as a representative of the social work profession, a professional social work organization, or the social worker's employing agency.

(b) Social workers who speak on behalf of professional social work organizations should accurately represent the official and authorized positions of the organizations.

(c) Social workers should ensure that their representations to clients, agencies, and the public of professional qualifications, credentials, education, competence, affiliations, services provided, or results to be achieved are accurate. Social workers should claim only those relevant professional credentials they actually possess and take steps to correct any inaccuracies or misrepresentations of their credentials by others.

4.07 Solicitations

(a) Social workers should not engage in uninvited solicitation of potential clients who, because of their circumstances, are vulnerable to undue influence, manipulation, or coercion.

(b) Social workers should not engage in solicitation of testimonial endorsements (including solicitation of consent to use a client's prior statement as a testimonial endorsement) from current clients or from other people who, because of their particular circumstances, are vulnerable to undue influence.

4.08 Acknowledging Credit

(a) Social workers should take responsibility and credit, including authorship credit, only for work they have actually performed and to which they have contributed.

(b) Social workers should honestly acknowledge the work of and the contributions made by others.

5. Social Workers' Ethical Responsibilities to the Social Work Profession

5.01 Integrity of the Profession

(a) Social workers should work toward the maintenance and promotion of high standards of practice.

(b) Social workers should uphold and advance the values, ethics, knowledge, and mission of the profession. Social workers should protect, enhance, and improve the integrity of the profession through appropriate study and research, active discussion, and responsible criticism of the profession.

(c) Social workers should contribute time and professional expertise to activities that promote respect for the value, integrity, and competence of the social work profession. These activities may include teaching, research, consultation, service, legislative testimony, presentations in the community, and participation in their professional organizations.

(d) Social workers should contribute to the knowledge base of social work and share with colleagues their knowledge related to practice, research, and ethics. Social workers should seek to con-tribute to the profession's literature and to share their knowledge at professional meetings and conferences.

(e) Social workers should act to prevent the unauthorized and unqualified practice of social work.

5.02 Evaluation and Research

(a) Social workers should monitor and evaluate policies, the implementation of programs, and practice interventions.

(b) Social workers should promote and facilitate evaluation and research to contribute to the development of knowledge.

(c) Social workers should critically examine and keep current with emerging knowledge relevant to social work and fully use evaluation and research evidence in their professional practice.

(d) Social workers engaged in evaluation or research should carefully consider possible consequences and should follow guidelines developed for the protection of evaluation and research participants. Appropriate institutional review boards should be consulted.

(e) Social workers engaged in evaluation or research should obtain voluntary and written informed consent from participants, when appropriate, without any implied or actual deprivation or penalty for refusal to participate; without undue inducement to participate; and with due regard for participants' well-being, privacy, and dignity. Informed consent should include information about the nature, extent, and duration of the participation requested and disclosure of the risks and benefits of participation in the research.

(f) When evaluation or research participants are incapable of giving informed consent, social workers should provide an appropriate explanation to the participants, obtain the participants' assent to the extent they are able, and obtain written consent from an appropriate proxy.

(g) Social workers should never design or conduct evaluation or research that does not use consent procedures, such as certain forms of naturalistic observation and archival research, unless rigorous and responsible review of the research has found it to be justified because of its prospective scientific, educational, or applied value and unless equally effective alternative procedures that do not involve waiver of consent are not feasible.

(h) Social workers should inform participants of their right to withdraw from evaluation and research at any time without penalty.

(I) Social workers should take appropriate steps to ensure that participants in evaluation and research have access to appropriate supportive services.

(j) Social workers engaged in evaluation or research should protect participants from unwarranted physical or mental distress, harm, danger, or deprivation.

(k) Social workers engaged in the evaluation of services should discuss collected information only for professional purposes and only with people professionally concerned with this information.

(l) Social workers engaged in evaluation or research should ensure the anonymity or confidentiality of participants and of the data obtained from them. Social workers should inform participants of any limits of confidentiality, the measures that will be taken to ensure confidentiality, and when any records containing research data will be destroyed.

(m) Social workers who report evaluation and research results should protect participants' confidentiality by omitting identifying information unless proper consent has been obtained authorizing disclosure.

(n) Social workers should report evaluation and research findings accurately. They should not fabricate or falsify results and should take steps to correct any errors later found in published data using standard publication methods.

(o) Social workers engaged in evaluation or research should be alert to and avoid conflicts of interest and dual relationships with participants, should inform participants when a real or potential conflict of interest arises, and should take steps to resolve the issue in a manner that makes participants' interests primary.

(p) Social workers should educate themselves, their students, and their colleagues about responsible research practices.

6. Social Workers' Ethical Responsibilities to the Broader Society

6.01 Social Welfare
Social workers should promote the general welfare of society, from local to global levels, and the development of people, their communities, and their environments. Social workers should advocate for living conditions conducive to the fulfillment of basic human needs and should promote social, economic, political, and cultural values and institutions that are compatible with the realization of social justice.

6.02 Public Participation
Social workers should facilitate informed participation by the public in shaping social policies and institutions.

6.03 Public Emergencies
Social workers should provide appropriate professional services in public emergencies to the greatest extent possible.

6.04 Social and Political Action
(a) Social workers should engage in social and political action that seeks to ensure that all people have equal access to the resources, employment, services, and opportunities they require to meet their basic human needs and to develop fully. Social workers should be aware of the impact of the political arena on practice and should advocate for changes in policy and legislation to improve social conditions in order to meet basic human needs and promote social justice.

(b) Social workers should act to expand choice and opportunity for all people, with special regard for vulnerable, disadvantaged, oppressed, and exploited people and groups.

(c) Social workers should promote conditions that encourage respect for cultural and social diversity within the United States and globally. Social workers should promote policies and practices that demonstrate respect for difference, support the expansion of cultural knowledge and resources, advocate for programs and institutions that demonstrate cultural competence, and promote policies that safeguard the rights of and confirm equity and social justice for all people.

(d) Social workers should act to prevent and eliminate domination of, exploitation of, and discrimination against any person, group, or class on the basis of race, ethnicity, national origin, color, sex, sexual orientation, age, marital status, political belief, religion, or mental or physical disability

For more information on Merrill Education products,
please visit our website at http://www.prenhall.com

PEARSON

Merrill
Prentice Hall

StudentAid.ed.gov
FUNDING YOUR FUTURE.

ISBN 0-13-239886-9

90000

9 780132 398862

RC 455.2 .E8 G85 2007

A guide to ethical conduct
for the helping profession